Skyline
2015

Cyberworld Publishing

www.CyberworldPublishing.com

This book is copyright © Olivia Stowe 2015
First published by Cyberworld Publishing in 2015
Cover design by S Bush © 2015
Cover photo: manipulated, Copyright: melis at Shutterstock
E-book ISBN: 978-1-922187-14-7
Print ISBN: 978-1-922187-81-9

Cyberworld Publishing
Jindalee St
Toronto, NSW, 2283
Australia

Skyline 2015

*An Anthology of
Prose and Poetry by
Central Virginia Writers*

Olivia Stowe, ed.

Table of Contents

Introduction   9

Prose Fiction

Cousin Barnaby Is Dead by Clifford Garstang   13
Gravity by Sarah Collins Honenberger   20
The Storm by Jean Lancaster   30
Lucky by Jean Lancaster   41
(Honorable mention fiction, Virginia Writers Club 2014
Summer Shorts Writing Contest)
Nun Run by Elaine Ruggieri   45
(First place fiction, Blue Ridge Writers VWC, 2014)
JFK, Daddy, and Me by Deborah M. Prum   55
(Second place fiction, Blue Ridge Writers VWC, 2014)
Brave Girl by Jody Hobbs Hesler   66
(Third place fiction, Blue Ridge Writers VWC 2014)
The Invisibles by Gary D. Kessler   72
The Magic Sweatshirt by Brenda A. Morris   81
Blue Christmas by Olivia Stowe   83

Poetry

Before Your Surgery by Sharon Leiter   95
I am running away from your body by Sharon Leiter   97
A Visit by Sharon Leiter   98
Garden Gems by Elizabeth Doyle Solomon   99
Sunday in Shenandoah by Elizabeth Doyle Solomon   100
Night Rain by Elizabeth Doyle Solomon   101
Howling Totem by Sigrid Mirabella   102
Heart of a Wolf by Sigrid Mirabella   103
Outfoxed by the Moon by Sigrid Mirabella   104
Famine Cottages, Ireland 2009 by Jody Hobbs Hesler   105
(First place poetry, Blue Ridge Writers VWC, 2014)

Shadows in the Sand by Linda Levokove 107
(*Second place poetry, Blue Ridge Writers VWC, 2014*)
My Child in the Moonlight by Linda Levokove 109
(*From* Cabbages & Kings)
Of Flesh and Roses by Linda Levokove 110
(*From* Cabbages & Kings)
Warring With Words by Lauvonda Lynn Young 111
(*Third place poetry, Blue Ridge Writers VWC, 2014*)
Planting Seeds by Leonard Tuchyner 112
(Echo Magazine; *from* A Journey to Elsewhere)
Morning Dove by Leonard Tuchyner 113

Prose Nonfiction

Close Encounters of the Furry Kind
by Susan M. Lanterman 117
Nana's Arm by Jean Lancaster 120
(*Second place nonfiction, Virginia Writers Club
2014 Summer Shorts Writing Contest*)
The Price of a Pig by Erin Newton Wells 124
(*First place nonfiction, Blue Ridge Writers VWC, 2014*)
My Dad's Last Gun by Jody Hobbs Hesler 131
(*Second place nonfiction, Blue Ridge Writers VWC, 2014*)
Light in the Forest by Phyllis R. Koch-Sheras 135
(*Third place nonfiction, Blue Ridge Writers VWC, 2014*)
My Father's World by Leonard Tuchyner 139
Death of a Friend by Gerry Kruger 148
Keeping in Touch and Finding Patience
by Gary D. Kessler 151

On Writing/Publishing

Liberating the Big Bat by Deborah M. Prum 157
Tip: How to Make Characters Lively
by Deborah M. Prum 159

**The Monkey and the Basket: A Lesson in Problem
   Solving** by Deborah M. Prum   161
Living With Our Muses by Jody Hobbs Hesler   163
The Joy of Writing Groups by Linda Levokove   165

About the Authors   169

Introduction

Skyline 2015, the second in a series of annual publisher's anthologies produced by Cyberworld Publishing, showcases the prose and poetry talents of Central Virginia writers. The title of the anthology is taken from the Skyline Drive, the parkway skipping along the top of the Blue Ridge Mountains in Virginia and providing centering for the region in which the authors showcased here are living and writing.

There is no overarching theme for the works in this anthology, so each can be discovered and appreciated for its own context and merits. Over half of the works found here are works by Central Virginia writers that ranked high in various writing contests during 2014. The foundation is the 2014 writing contest of the Blue Ridge Writers Chapter of the Virginia Writers Club. Also included in the anthology are other works selected from the portfolios of these contest selectees, special contributor works by established writers in the region, and poems from recently published works by Central Virginia writers.

The anthology consists of thirty-nine works by nineteen authors in four sections: fiction, poetry, nonfiction, and, since this is a writer's anthology, a section on writing and publishing. Eclectic is the hallmark word for this collection. Many of the authors here are purposely represented by more than one work in varied media to showcase their writing skills. Notably, Jody Hobbs Hesler took honors in all three categories of the Blue Ridge Writers 2014 contest, all of which are included in this anthology—the short story "Brave Girl," the poem "Famine Cottages, Ireland 2009," and the essay "My Dad's Last Gun"—but also provides the writing advice essay, "Living with Our Muses."

The fiction section leads off with "Cousin Barnaby Is Dead," telling of the complications of a death notice, by Clifford Garstang, winner of the 2013 Library of Virginia Literary Award for Fiction. Noted regional poet, Sharon Leiter, leads the poetry section with a trilogy of poems on the passing of a spouse. Charlottesville *Daily Progress* features writer Susan M. Lanterman contributes an essay in a series of experiences on opening a Charlottesville B&B in the nonfiction section's "Close Encounters of the Furry Kind." And prolific writer in various media, Deborah M. Prum, provides a trio of short writing advice essays to open the "On Writing/Publishing" section.

A notable additional section to this anthology is the "About the Authors" section, which provides fascinating, I think, literary background notes on the authors represented in this collection. Be sure not to miss the extensive and rich writing experience of our authors. I'm sure you will be as impressed with their accomplishments as I have been.

As with the initial *Skyline 2014*, it has been a delight to work with and read the many varied themes and enjoy the high quality of writing of these Central Virginia writers, many of whom were published to the marketplace in the past year. I hope you will find these works as fresh and as entertaining and thought provoking as I have. These indeed are exceptional writers who deserve to have their works highlighted and represented in the marketplace.

Olivia Stowe
Volume Editor
Skyline 2015

PROSE FICTION

Cousin Barnaby Is Dead

Clifford Garstang

I'm in the middle of an argument with my mother—she thinks I should ask her friend's daughter, Denise Knickerbocker, out on a date while I'm home for spring break, and I think that's the worst idea ever—when the phone rings. I want her to let the answering machine get it, or make Dad answer it, wherever he is, in their bedroom or the basement or sneaking a smoke on the back porch, because I want her to listen to me for a change. Instead, she glances at the caller ID and lifts the receiver.

After "Hello," she's silent, nods solemnly as if the caller can see her and will understand that she's taking whatever it is seriously. Then it's "Yes," "Yes," "I'm so sorry," and she hangs up. She looks at me and there are tears in her eyes.

"Cousin Barnaby is dead." She says this with resignation in her voice, as if the news is inevitable.

I don't know what to say. It doesn't seem possible. The guy's my age, but he's *her* first cousin, the son of her mother's younger sister. The first time I met him was at a family reunion in Cleveland that I did *not* want to go to and neither did he. We were maybe twelve at the time. I was missing basketball camp back home in Indianapolis, and Barn—he liked to be called Barn, but his parents insisted on the whole dumb name that made him sound like a circus clown—was into hanging out with his friends at the mall in Pittsburgh. So we were both there against our wills. Another time was here in Indy just a couple of years ago when Barn and his mother came to visit. I think she was getting a divorce or something and wanted to hide out for a while. I remember there was a big hubbub because Barn's older brother Bailey didn't come with them. He was supposed to be some hotshot college guy, which back then seemed like a big deal. It was cool that he didn't come, though, because Barn brought some pot he stole from Bailey's bedroom, and we smoked out in the woods behind our house. He talked about Hermann Hesse and alienation and duality and more shit that was way over my head. I thought he was cool.

Cousin Barnaby is dead. Shit.

"How?" I ask my mother.

She doesn't answer.

Even though we didn't see each other much, now that I'm thinking about him I feel pretty bad that he's dead. I don't know anyone my age who's dead, except this kid in high school who had some horrible disease and scooted around the school in an electric wheelchair so no one would feel guilty about not wanting to talk to him. So I didn't *really* know him. When he died, the school set up a scholarship in his name. I didn't hear who got the scholarship—other kids in wheelchairs, maybe.

"Never mind, Robbie," my mother says, finally, like she's been thinking all this time of what lie to tell me.

If she doesn't want to talk about it, I'm guessing either Barn killed himself, which doesn't seem possible, or maybe somebody killed him, and either way it sucks. It's lame that she won't tell me, but typical for her. My folks think I'm still a kid and can't handle the truth.

I must have rolled my eyes then because she does an about-face, which is pretty unusual for her.

"If you must know, it was an accident. He was driving his little Korean car or Yugo or whatever and he crashed. Died instantly. Are you happy now?"

Of course I'm not happy. What a crazy thing to say! That would be creepy under any circumstances, although I *am* glad she decided to tell me, which says something about where we are in our relationship. Maybe it's because I'm a college man now. We're making progress.

Anyway, our argument is over now thanks to Barn. I can see she's forgotten about Denise Knickerbocker, and instead she's thinking about how awful her aunt must feel and what a relief it is that it happened to her pothead cousin and not her own son. She doesn't notice that I'm holding on to the back of a chair so I don't fall over. I can't believe Barn is dead. I didn't even know he had a car.

The real reason I don't want to ask Denise out, by the way, and the reason we were arguing in the first place, is because of the nickname some guys used to call her behind her back: DeNeeds Biggerknockers. After I heard that once, I couldn't even look at her, never mind go out on a date with her. Can you imagine trying to feel her up and having that name come to mind? I wouldn't be able to keep a straight face.

But now, after Mom's shocker, there *is* somebody I want to see. This girl named Corinne Ackerman had a huge crush on Barn, the kind where you write somebody love poems and send them e-mails and threaten to do terrible things to yourself if they don't write back. She met him when he was here that one time, and I think they might have made out when I wasn't around. I'm pretty sure they stayed in touch after that, because once when I talked to Barn on the phone he mentioned he could have Corinne any time he wanted. He even talked about what he'd like to do with her. It was kind of crude, but funny. Anyway, I figure she's home for spring break just like I am, and this is news she'd want to have.

After dinner, my folks start talking about driving to Pittsburgh for Barn's funeral, which seems like the worst thing imaginable. I mean, I really liked the guy, like I said, and it's sad and everything that he got killed, but there's no way I'm going to his funeral and looking into a coffin at his dead face. He was a good-looking kid, you know, and when he said those things about having sex with Corinne any time he wanted, he wasn't joking. And not just Corinne, but any girl he set his sights on. I don't want to even think about going to the funeral.

So I tell my parents I'm meeting some buddies—we're all home for spring break and we're going to hang out, I say, although the truth is a bunch of them went to Cabo or someplace and I'm stuck here in Indianapolis where there's still snow on the ground. Besides I'm not really in the mood for hanging out with guys who didn't know Barn. Instead, I head over to Corinne Ackerman's.

Corinne's mom is shocked to see me because it's been a couple of years, but after a double-take she invites me in and says what a nice surprise and Corinne will be so happy. Then she calls down the hall. Speaking of surprises, I'm floored when Corinne comes out. I used to think Barn was making fun of her when he talked about doing it with her because she was kind of chubby when we were younger. Now she's incredibly skinny. Like way too skinny.

We sit in the living room and Corinne's mom serves us Coke and pretzels—although what I really want at this point is a beer—and says again what a nice surprise it is to see me.

"How's Barnaby?" Corinne asks as soon as we're alone, and I can tell she hasn't gotten over the thing she had for him, and it might not be so easy to tell her what I've come to tell her.

"You home for break?" I ask, because that's what my dad does. Whenever I ask a question he doesn't want to answer, he just asks another question.

"No," she says. "I mean, I'm on break, but I didn't go away. I'm in school here."

Corinne was near the top of our class, took all the advanced courses. I figured she'd have gone to Harvard or someplace. Notre Dame, at least.

"That's convenient," I say.

"So how's Barnaby?" she asks again.

I sip the Coke, munch a couple of pretzels. I can hear the TV going in the living room where her mom is, some sitcom with a loud laugh track.

"That's the thing, Cor," I say, putting on this fake nickname-closeness I don't really feel, "I've got some bad news about Barn."

The color leaves her face, and I can see her shoulders stiffen, like she's preparing to get slugged. I reach for another pretzel, but there's no way I can stop now. So I just say it.

"Barnaby is dead."

It starts slowly, so there's time for her to put down her drink, but she begins to shake all over. First her head trembles, and then I see her long hair kind of dancing around on her shoulders because her whole body is quivering. Her hand flies to her mouth and she's bending over like she's going to vomit. She jumps off the couch and runs to the bathroom, and I can hear it, probably what little dinner she ate is coming back up. Of course she knows all about puking, I figure, so for her this is probably no big deal.

When I go to tell Mrs. Ackerman that Corinne's sick, she's already standing outside the bathroom looking tired, like she's done this one too many times. I can hear Corinne inside sobbing and puking, so I tell her mom that I have to go, and I get out of there as fast as I can. Telling her was supposed to make me feel better, but instead I feel a hundred times worse.

I can't go home, though. I told my folks I'm hanging out with buddies, and it's too early for that to be over. And, besides, I don't want to hear any more about the funeral or that Barn must have been doing drugs, or whatever. So I walk around the neighborhood for a while. It's nothing special, nothing but single-story ranch houses, pretty much the same as when I was a kid. I get in the car and drive past our house once to check, and the lights are still on, so I go on down to the McDonald's near the interstate, which is just about the lamest thing I could possibly do, and I eat a hamburger I don't even want, try not to think about Barn, and then drive around some more. When I make another pass by the house it's dark, so I figure it's safe to head in.

When I get to my room, I'm feeling pretty low. For one thing, seeing Corinne was weird. She's obviously got some problems, but I didn't think she'd take the news about Barn that hard. Or maybe I did, and that's why I went over there. But the thing that bothers me is that it hit her way harder than it did me, and he's my cousin for Christ's sake. But, now that I think about it, the whole thing does really suck, and I wish Barn weren't dead. I never got to tell him I thought he was cool and, you know, that I liked him. Not that he cared what his dorky cousin from Indiana thought, but still. And then, out of no place, I start to cry. Not like Corinne, who was completely out of control, but a few tears sneak out of the corners of my eyes and run down my cheeks.

After a while the tears stop, but I'm not sure they're gone for good, like when you think you've put an end to a spell of hiccups, but back they come.

And then I think of this guy Roy I know at school. We were shooting the breeze one day in the dorm cafeteria and I found out he's from Pittsburgh, so I asked him if he knew Barnaby Mackintosh. "Sure I know him," he said. It turns out they went to the same high school. So, mostly because he knew Barn and even claimed to be friends with him, I started hanging out with Roy sometimes. He's a pretty good guy—smart but not so smart he makes you feel bad about yourself, pretty interested in girls but not so successful that you feel like a loser around him. That's Roy. I really want to talk to someone about Barn and how I feel about him. That's the real reason I went over to see Corinne, I realize, but that hadn't gone so well. If I could talk to Roy and we could both tell each other what a great guy Barn was, then we'll make ourselves feel better and we'll be honoring Barn in some way too, and that'll be better than some lousy funeral any day.

The phone's in the living room, so I go back out there. It takes awhile to get his folks' number from directory assistance, but then I call. It's late and I'm worried about that, but it's not something that's going to wait until tomorrow, not the way I'm feeling, so I let the phone ring and ring and finally somebody picks it up.

"Roy," I say, because I recognize his voice. "It's Robbie. How're you doing?"

Great, he says, or something like that, but honestly I'm not listening. I'm figuring out what I'm going to say next, and I'm trying really hard not to cry.

"Look, Roy, the reason I'm calling is I just heard that my cousin Barnaby is dead."

There's silence on his end of the line and I figure the news is sinking in. I know it's a tough thing to hear.

"No, he's not," says Roy. He's in denial. Totally understandable. I'm about to lose it again myself.

"Yeah, he is," I say. "Somebody called my mom. He had an accident or something. Barn's dead."

"I'm telling you he's not. I *just* saw him at a party. He was getting seriously wasted because his brother got killed in a wreck. It's Bailey that's dead, man. Not Barn."

Holy shit. Did my mom confuse the names? Did she mean Bailey, not Barnaby? Or did whoever called her get it wrong? Did I hear it wrong?

The first thing I think of is Corinne. I've never seen anyone so hung up on another person, and I guess she had problems of her own to deal with besides. People like that are on the edge, you know? But maybe it's okay. When I left her house she was with her mom. She probably talks stuff over with her, not like me and my mom, and if the news of Barn's death upset her that bad her mother would help her out.

Even so, I have to tell her about the mix-up. Only I don't want my folks to hear the car starting up again, and since it's just a couple of blocks away I head outside. It's cold as hell, and I don't have a jacket on, but I don't want to take the time to go back inside and get one, so I just start jogging and figure I'll warm up pretty quick.

And as I'm running, I feel myself start to smile, laugh even, because cousin Barnaby isn't dead after all. It was just a crazy mix-up with my mom. I feel bad about Bailey, of course, but I hardly even knew him, and I'm thinking that tomorrow I'll call Barn in Pittsburgh, and I guess I won't tell him what happened but I'll tell him how sorry I am about his brother and stuff, and it will be great to hear his voice. Maybe we can meet up this summer, spend some time together.

So I'm running down the street, I'm grinning and pretty happy about how things have turned out considering how shitty I felt a little while ago, and I'm watching the road because like I said it's cold and there's snow on the ground and black icy patches on the pavement that will send me flying if I hit one. And that's why I don't see the ambulance in front of Corinne's house until I'm practically on top of it. It's a wonder how I could have missed it, because the red light on top is spinning and flashing and spreading that eerie light all over the neighborhood.

I look up and I see Corinne's mom standing in their doorway. She's crying and her hand is covering her mouth, and there's some man standing there with her like he's asking questions. I know, as sure as I know anything, what happened.

And I also know that I am the last person Mrs. Ackerman wants to see right now. So I just keep on running, past the ambulance, past the house, through the cold dark neighborhood of my childhood, in the spooky glow of that flashing light.

Gravity

Sarah Collins Honenberger

When Bev heard the front door open and shut, she called down the stairs, "Hey, Maury. D'you bring the mail?" A gust of cold air raced past her and she shivered. Winter had lasted too long this year. She was so ready for those cheerful little snowdrops to poke up through the hoary ground and announce that warmer weather was coming.

Maury dropped the briefcase by the umbrella stand and headed straight for the liquor cabinet. Every time he drew his right foot forward, he hesitated slightly before setting it down. It reminded her of that children's story where the bear has a thorn in his paw. Was it the mouse who finally saved the bear? She couldn't remember.

While Maury opened the cupboard and clinked the bottles around, he called back to her. "Four o'clock in the post office is a mob scene. I'll go after dinner."

"We have to check the apartment too. The new tenant wants to move in this weekend, and I haven't been there since Leonard moved out."

"Leonard moved out?" He was joking.

It had taken them almost two months to convince Leonard to leave. It had required daily consultations with him, at first one or the other of them on the telephone, eventually in tandem and in person. Two years ago Leonard had wangled his way into the apartment with a sob story about downsizing and an ex-wife and a revolutionary invention that just needed some intensive investment of quiet time. Bev, the creative one, had sympathized. Maury, seeing the softening of her frown, had simply scratched through the typed lease with the changes she suggested. *The only thing to do*, she said, in light of Leonard's obvious depression. They'd allowed him to spread the deposit over two months and to pay less than the previous tenant for the first year.

Maury's warning aside, the reduced rent had eventually dwindled into no rent and convoluted written treatises from

Leonard on the evils of accumulated wealth. It had taken the threat of legal action before he had finally agreed to pack up his odd collection of thrift store clothes and computer equipment and disappear.

Maury eyed her over the drink as if he were contemplating a toast. "I thought you went over last week?"

"I was working on a story."

"Ah, of course. Writing's more important than eating."

"You creep. You could've gone yourself if it was so damn important."

Maury kissed her—smack, smack—his lips sweet with the sour mash. "Let's walk over after dinner. Supposed to be shooting stars tonight."

"I haven't started dinner."

"I'll do it."

Bev poured herself a glass of wine and traipsed back upstairs to the glowing computer screen. She might have time to finish this chapter. Sitting in the straight-back chair where she'd spent the afternoon, she typed sporadically, mostly mused. You couldn't just spit out a novel. You had to think and arrange things in your head.

No one understood, not Maury, not her mother, neither of her sons. Writing fiction took a lot of time. Some of the most successful writers said they were lucky if they wrote five pages a day. On a good day she could write ten. Her writing friends loved these characters, this story, so she must be doing something right. It was the publishers she had to convince. Well, first an agent.

Directly below the study she heard water running in the kitchen, some pounding, a whirl of banging, and a fine-tuned whining. It must be the blender. In spite of Maury's comments about production—his business school background made him think dollars first—he supported her writing. More than merely funding a lifestyle that allowed her not to have a paycheck job, he listened to what she shared, made suggestions, and marveled at the good parts. She sipped the wine, then read back over the last couple of paragraphs.

Her protagonist was a little flakier than she'd intended. Sometimes the characters did that all by themselves—distanced themselves from her in unexpected ways, the same way her sons had done. Emmett lived half way across the country in Salt Lake City, unmarried, but making a name for himself as an environmental engineer. At least that's what he said in his weekly telephone calls. It wasn't that she didn't believe him. It was just that it was not easy to verify, and she wondered why he was driving the same old Volvo he'd had in college if he was so sought after in engineering circles.

Daniel, Emmett's much younger brother, was very different. He spent months at a time with them. He would drag around, berating the latest girlfriend or employer who never understood him until Maury put his foot down and Daniel would find another job. They would move him and his stuff, always within a two-hundred-mile radius of their house. She'd buy a week's worth of groceries, and they wouldn't see him for a year.

She reread the last paragraph again. Smells from the kitchen seeped through the floorboards of the house with the February chill. She slid off the chair and found a pair of Maury's wool ski socks in the laundry basket and put them on over her own socks. If they were walking to the apartment, she'd need a heavier sweater. She rummaged in the closet.

"Virginia Woolf, I presume?" Maury announced. His tie hung loose from the open collar, his shoes in his hand. He was grinning.

She smiled back.

"Dinner's ready." He leaned down to look at what she'd been writing. After blinking his eyes several times in front of the computer, he shook his head.

"You don't like it?" she asked.

"I must need new glasses. It's all blurry."

"It's the whiskey."

"Oh, good," he chuckled, "You just saved me hundreds of dollars."

* * * *

Even the stars looked frozen in the frosty night. There was not a single cloud, no moon. They walked slowly, mostly, she thought, from the wine.

"What's with your foot?" she asked.

"What's the matter with my foot?"

"You're favoring the left one. Like you stepped on a shell and cut yourself."

Maury didn't answer. With his head tipped backwards, he gazed into the sky. "It's damn cold out here. I hope he's really gone."

"Leonard?"

"Who else?"

"Well, I thought he was packing when you were there at Christmas."

"He was, but there was still a lot of junk around. Plus, you know Leonard. He could live out of boxes if his plans fell through and he had nowhere else to go."

She began to dread their arrival. The apartment was only three blocks from the house. When the condo unit had come up for foreclosure, they'd bought it cheap. One year Daniel lived in it when he had a local job. Maury believed real estate investments were the best, but she hated the frantic phone calls when the furnace conked out or the disposal backed up. That had been one nice thing about Leonard. The little things never bothered him. He had bigger issues to confront.

No lights were on, a good sign. While she stamped her snowy feet on the mat, Maury unlocked the door. There were two mountainous garbage bags of trash in the front hall. Tenants were so lazy.

Once they'd inspected the kitchen and started for the bedroom, they both noticed the smell at the same moment. Maury strode ahead of her, but halted at the bathroom door.

"Smells like a dead animal," she said.

"You wish."

The medicine cabinet mirror was snowy with toothpaste. Over his shoulder when he bent forward, she could see the toilet, a horrid brown muck.

"Gawd," she stepped back and turned away so she wouldn't have to see it.

He flushed it, but the familiar whir of water racing downwards didn't follow. There was a sick sluggish gurgle, then Maury's curses under his breath.

"Where's the friggin' plunger? That pea brain took the plunger."

Bev tried to remember whether she'd bought a plunger for this bathroom. They had two at home—one by each toilet. She raced to the kitchen, flung open the cupboard under the kitchen sink, and peered in. Except for the puddle of green slime under the drainpipe, there was nothing. He'd taken her rubber gloves. The man must have a fetish. In all these months she'd never seen him cleaning. He hadn't even called to ask about Laundromats until the second month. She should have known.

While she was checking the hall closet, Maury shouted. "Bev, I need the plunger. Bev."

Checking under and around the furniture they'd rented with the space, she passed through the living room, noticed the stack of porn videos, and shuddered. You never really knew anyone. On the tiny porch, suspended above the ski slope, she found the plunger, hanging upside down in a mangled metal clothes hanger. When she tugged it loose, a chunk of frozen ice flew out and smashed on the concrete. For all she knew, Leonard could have been measuring rainfall for one of his kooky inventions.

"I'm coming," she yelled back to Maury, who was still bellowing obscenities.

The smell was overpowering. She couldn't stay to watch him. Back on the patio, she sucked in the fresh air and wondered if her boys ever took the time to look at the stars. Poor Maury. It had been his idea to take this nice peaceful walk and Leonard had intruded his cruddy personality one last time. She should be helping.

While Maury fought the toilet monster, she dragged the trash bags out to the landing and contemplated the best way to maneuver two flights of stairs. The elevator was carpeted and she hated to risk leaving an indelible odor there, if one of the bags sprung a hole.

"Hello," a bright voice spoke above her head. Bev looked up the stairwell at a young woman with a reddish Afro.

24

"Hello," Bev answered.

"You haven't seen Ricky, have you?"

"Ricky?"

"He lived there, in that apartment you're moving into."

"I don't think so, Leonard Massimo lived here."

"Ricky lived with Leonard."

"Oh," Bev said. The queasy feeling in her gut tightened into anger. "Whoever the hell Ricky is, he's not here, but he left his . . . ah, garbage."

The redhead stepped back out of sight. "Jeez, lady, you don't have to be so ugly about it."

Maury appeared, disheveled and red-faced. "Who are you talking to?"

"Some girl upstairs. She was asking about Ricky."

"Who the hell is Ricky?"

Bev found the mop under the bed. She hated to think how it had ended up there. After she mopped the floor and put the mop out on the balcony to air, they locked up. Walking home, they held hands, despite their ski gloves.

"Sorry about that," she said.

"How could he do that to you? You contributed to his fundraiser for endangered animals."

"Never mind. It's over. Let's stop for the mail."

The ski village post office was empty. Low wattage bulbs made the corridor, lined with metal boxes and Most Wanted posters, seem more depressing than normal. Maury extricated the key from his pants pocket and, without looking, he wadded the envelopes into his parka, zippering them inside the front pouch of his jacket.

"D'you call your mom to tell her we're coming through next month?"

"I forgot."

"Did you call the accountant about the taxes?"

"Yes," she crowed, knowing full well he had expected another failure. She deserved it. The telephone was her adversary, waiting in ambush, brazen and confident that she was too chicken to stop and dial. She hated the phone. That had been part of the problem with Leonard. "I'll call tomorrow. I promise."

She could feel the heat from Maury's body, even in the wintry air. After this walk, they could've gone home and stripped for a communal shower, snuggled by the fire, and fallen asleep in each other's arms. If Leonard hadn't interjected the chaos of his life once again. The image of the overflowing toilet wouldn't go away. And who the hell was Ricky anyway?

Because Maury went straight to the shower without a kiss, Bev stayed in the kitchen. While she waited for the kettle to whistle, she removed the mail from his jacket. One by one, she slit the envelopes and laid out the contents. The New York City address stopped her. It was the agent who had agreed to consider her first book. A thin envelope, definitely not a contract. They really knew how to pick their weapon. She read it three times. According to this stranger, the manuscript lacked narrative tension and the characters were not consistent or credible. It needed editing.

"Damn," she said, "Damn, damn, damn."

Above her head, the shower stopped draining inside the ceiling. Her turn. She went up. When she passed Maury in the bedroom. She swatted his rear.

"Feel better?" she asked.

He grunted and disappeared into the closet.

She ran the bath as hot as she could stand it. Lying in that pulsing heat, with her head back and wine glass shadows grazing the white walls, the sad evening hovered in the shadows of her consciousness. Like a great bear, Maury puttered around on the other side of the door, then sank onto the squeaky bed. He snored almost instantly.

She dissected the sentences in the agent's letter. The problem, she decided, was that island life, what she'd written, didn't appeal to big city people, execs who liked the fast pace. The slow rhythm of the beach and the sun—margaritas and mangoes—that life was too foreign for them to understand. She didn't need to rewrite. She needed an agent from St. Thomas.

When the water cooled, she toweled off, dressed in a flannel nightgown and another pair of Maury's fuzzy socks, and returned to the computer. The phone rang. She rushed to answer it so it wouldn't wake up Maury.

"Beverly? Why are you up so late?"

"It's only eleven, Mom."

"So what are you two lovebirds up to?"

"Maury's asleep. I'm writing."

"Ach, you ought to be in bed with that man. Such a nice man. I like him."

"Me too, Mom. But the agent wrote today, and . . .well, it's not good news."

"They don't want it?"

It was amazing how quickly her mother could make her feel like she was seven again, muddy fingerprints on the wall.

"Beverly? Were you going to tell me what the agent said?"

"Well, she said it had some problems."

"I don't know why you're writing a novel anyway. I read an article about a woman who won a million dollars from Betty Crocker. With a recipe. Why don't you just write a recipe?"

Bev groaned. "Is that what you called to tell me, Mom?"

"Of course not, but you brought it up, about the writing and all. I wanted you to know that Emmett called and he sounds fine."

"Thanks, I just talked with him Sunday."

"So you're glad he's engaged to Judith."

Bev sputtered, groped for the wine glass on the side table, and gulped the rest.

"Sure, sure," she answered, "Good news, eh?"

Her mother was uncharacteristically silent. Bev imagined her standing with one hand on her hip, staring her down the way she used to in high school when Bev appeared at the breakfast table with a skirt that was too short.

"You like her?" her mother asked.

"We don't even know her, but if Emmett likes her, that's fine with us."

"Hmmph," her mother was breathing heavily into the receiver.

"I gotta go, Mom, I'm in the middle of something."

"Fine, fine. I am sorry about the agent. You were always a good cook."

Bev felt like crying. Instead she threw the fourteenth edition of the *Chicago Manual of Style* into the trashcan. She'd better call Emmett. She always called him at the office, but, if he were engaged, he wouldn't be working this late. He'd be with her. Judith.

She couldn't find her purse. With Emmett's home number. "Damn," she muttered, not feeling any better. She checked the stairway post. She yanked closet doors wide and eyed unlit corners. It wasn't in the living room or on the dining room chair where she often left it.

"That agent is an idiot," she mumbled. "She just wants steamy sex scenes, someone famous doing it with a minority drug addict. She doesn't care about careful, well-thought-out prose."

She raked her hand under the sofa. No purse. On tiptoes in the bedroom so she didn't wake Maury, she checked her bureau drawers. No purse. She must have left it at Leonard's. She pulled her jeans up under her nightgown and crept downstairs again. In the front hall she laced her hiking boots over the heavy socks. She let the door close gently and stomped off across yesterday's snow.

In the apartment she buried her nose in the scarf while she retraced her steps. "Leonard, you little creep. You and your stupid ideas and your illicit roommate. Ricky, schticky. If you think you're getting that deposit back after the toilet stunt, hah." But the purse was not there either.

Stumbling back to the house in the dark, she seethed. The wind cut right through her layers. In those three blocks she could have become an ice sculpture. When the key wouldn't turn the lock, she guessed the tumbler was frozen. She blew on it several times and tried again. By the time she managed to open it, she was bawling.

Maury found her on the sofa, her shoulders heaving. "Babe, what's going on?"

"I can't find my purse. I've looked everywhere. I thought I left it at the apartment, but it's gone. And that guy Ricky, whoever the hell he is, has a key. By now he's probably charging things all over town with my credit cards."

"I thought I heard the phone."

"My mother called to tell me I ought to be writing recipes."

He looked at her crooked, started to smile, but didn't after all.

"Poor Bevvy. Come here."

He held her to him. Through the flannel she could feel his heart thumping, slow, steady. Hers flopped wildly. She concentrated on aligning hers with his. She tried not to think about the purse and the agent and her flaky protagonist.

"I'm sorry about the mess in the apartment," she mumbled.

"Shhhh."

"Do you think Leonard and Ricky were . . . ?"

"Shhhh."

"Emmett's engaged, and he told Mom and not us."

"Shhhh."

"I always leave my purse on that chair."

She pointed and without letting go of each other, they both turned to look. The black leather strap gleamed in the pale light of the stars.

"Shhhh," Maury said, like he meant it.

The Storm

Jean Lancaster

Mary Margaret: 1935

The memories of the summer I turned thirteen live vividly in frightening dreams that wake me in the night. The summer of 1935 our servant Frederick disappeared in a torrential storm that pulsed across the mile-wide expanse of the Rappahannock River.

After that day my mother drifted into dark moods of soul-draining depression, rambling monologues, and abrupt departures from the house for hours. Our housemaid and cook, Hattie, tried her best to make our routines normal, but the loss of Frederick formed a cloud of secrets that Hattie carried in her heart. While my two younger brothers maintained their boyhood innocence, I tossed aside the charades of my childhood.

I was born when Mother was eighteen, exactly nine months after she and my father got married. They christened me Mary Margaret. And that's what everyone called me, but secretly I always wanted to be Maggie. I thought perhaps it would free me from our Southern rituals of double names and my Irish-Catholic behavior.

As I grew up, I thought my mother, Lillian, was the prettiest woman I had ever seen. She was beautiful, with reddish-brown hair worked into a French braid and twisted into a bun at the nape of her neck. Her eyes glistened like emeralds.

My father, Larkin Fitzpatrick, like Mother, was of Irish descent. I once looked up his first name in a library book about family names and found it meant rough and fierce. He was a gruff man who rarely showed any signs of love toward us. I noticed he acted especially ill mannered to our hired help.

Besides the yardman and housemaid at our Monument Avenue home in Richmond, my father hired Hattie's much younger, seventeen-year-old brother, Frederick, as chauffeur. He drove us to school and took Mother on her shopping trips. He took Father to the Dairy Bar for breakfast every morning, to and from work downtown, and to the Country Club of Virginia for dinner in the evenings. Father was rarely home for a family dinner. It seemed to me his work was more important than our family was.

Hattie took care of Mother when she was growing up. Now Hattie took care of my brothers and me, and that was besides all the cooking and cleaning, serving at Mother's luncheons and teas, and the laundry, and ironing. It seemed like a lot to do. I rarely saw her sit and rest.

Ever since we were little we called her Hattie instead of her given name, Harriet, since that was how the syllables curled out of our baby mouths. She was so short that by the time we were in upper elementary, we were tall enough to pat the top of her curly black-haired head. Her dark, wrinkled skin seemed to shine like a coffee bean in the sunlight.

When Frederick first started working for Father, he was never Freddy or Fred, but just the very quiet, respectful, and polite Frederick. The Negroes liked to honor their heroes, like Frederick Douglass and Harriet Tubman, when naming their children. Hattie said Frederick had not been to school except for a few years when he was about six years old. He grew up working on the tobacco farm that was one of many properties my grandfather owned besides being a country doctor. Hattie told me my grandmother taught Frederick to read and write some phrases from the Bible.

In 1935 the news reported that the aftermath of the Great Depression resonated throughout the United States. Our family was not affected as much as others in the capital city. When Mother took us downtown Saturday mornings to Thalhimer's Tea Room on Broad Street, we passed the yellowed fields of an expansive horse farm that stood empty. We also drove by the Methodist Children's Home that sheltered those whose families were stricken by poverty.

Mother said Father managed his money well, but I heard whisperings at school that he was in liquor sales with the fathers of my friends since prohibition had been repealed. He opened two new businesses that year, including a grand ballroom decorated with burgundy velvet, gilded sconces, and a roof that rolled open to a view of the constellations. The dance hall drew local residents and soldiers stationed in the area who were looking for escape from everyday life.

Father was doing so well he built a large, two-story house on the Rappahannock River. It was near Ware's Wharf, where lots of families we knew owned summer homes.

∗ ∗ ∗ ∗

After classes at our Catholic school ended in late May of 1935, we went to the river house for the first time. Frederick drove our father's brand-new Chevrolet Suburban. Hattie made the fifty-mile trip sitting atop a leather trunk that held our sheets, towels, and blankets. The entire time she held tight to the straps with her eyes closed against the bright sun that heated the windows.

When we arrived at the river, Frederick parked under the broad sycamore tree near the house. He pulled open the polished chrome handle of the heavy back door so that Mother and I could ease out across the middle seat. My brothers crawled over the front seat and leapt out the open door.

"Miss Hattie, give me your hand and I'll help you down," Frederick said. She must have weighed no more than the eighty-pound burlap sack of potatoes that Grandfather would bring us from his farm.

Frederick carried Mother's luggage inside to one of the first-floor bedrooms. He carried our smaller suitcases up the narrow stairs to the open attic bedroom. My brothers and I were amazed at how big it was, with its towering ceiling. The boys jumped from one to the other of the six single beds. We decided to call this our "Orphanage," because it was so like all the beds lined up in a row in the stories about Little Orphan Annie in the comic strip and the movie that we had seen.

Upstairs, I watched Frederick open all the double-sash dormer windows that jutted out of the peaked roof. His chest puffed out as he breathed in the cool brackish air blowing in from the river. From the other side of the room there was a view across the road of an old barn, a herd of cows, and grain silos.

From that window, I watched Hattie as she walked, slow and hunched over, carrying one full box of food at a time from the car to the kitchen. I could see Frederick carry all the rockers and wicker chairs around to the screened porch that spanned the width of the house facing the river. When he took Hattie's small brown satchel into the maid's quarters, I ran downstairs and slipped behind a tree to peek through the window. The bedroom was long and narrow, perhaps no more than eight footsteps wide. The only furniture was a wrought-iron bed covered with a hand-sewn quilt and a painted three-drawer dresser. A small oval mirror hung on a nail. I shivered when I saw it was discolored in ghostly patterns on the front of the silver-backed glass.

I heard Frederick knock on the back door leading to the kitchen and call to my mother, "Missus Lillian? Is there be anything else you like me to take care of? Are you ready for me to open all the kitchen windows for some fresh air?"

"Yes, Frederick. That would be nice. And, would you see if Hattie needs any help?" Mother answered from her bedroom.

"Yes, ma'am," he answered and entered the kitchen.

"Well, well, Sistah. You unpacked everything already. Did you forget? I told you, you should wait for me to help," he said.

"Now, Frederick, I ain't so old yet that I need help with my work." She laughed for the first time that day.

"I know that, just doin' what the Missus asked me to do. If you be alright, I think I'll tidy up the yard of all those sticks came down in the storm that come down the river," he said.

"Thanks for helpin'," Hattie replied.

I ran back around to the porch and settled on the cushioned wicker couch and listened to the osprey babies shriek. I tried hard to see their white-feathered heads pop up in the nest on roof of the next boathouse upriver. I heard Hattie move through the house as she pulled off the sheets that covered new furniture that had been delivered. After she fluffed up the pillows on the sofa and overstuffed chairs in the living room, she headed for the three bedrooms on the first floor and then up to the attic bedroom with fresh linens for the beds.

After we were all settled into the river house for the week, Frederick drove back to Richmond. That week Mother spent every day out on the porch reading paperback novels and sipping what looked to be tomato juice. I snuck a sip once when she was inside. It tasted like Father's breath smelled when he came home at night.

My brothers and I swam a lot and caught crabs with strings tied around raw chicken parts. We hooped and hollered when they got loose and scurried around the pier.

Hattie watched over us while we played in the brownish water close to the riverbank.

She brought our lunch out to the porch every day at noon. There were BLTs on toast for Mother and PBJs on Sunbeam bread for us. There was always a platter of paprika-sprinkled deviled eggs and a colander of fresh-picked and pitted cherries from the trees in the yard. After lunch, naptime was for everyone, except for Hattie, who took her turn on the porch and watched the ospreys and seagulls as they scooped fish out of the river.

That first week Frederick brought Father down on Friday evening. He settled his luggage in the master bedroom and set up the bar of Kentucky whiskey and sweet vermouth beside the living room fireplace. Saturday night Frederick set off fireworks that sprinkled the river with starlight. Sunday morning he drove our family to mass at St. Timothy's in the town of Tappahannock.

After church, we had a rare family dinner. Hattie dipped fresh-caught catfish and river bass in cornmeal and fried them up golden and crisp. She stirred up a batch of cornbread, added split and scraped corn kernels into the thick batter, and baked the bread in a heavy cast-iron skillet. She sliced up juicy Hanover tomatoes and simmered a kettle of green beans and fatty chunks of Virginia country ham that had been delivered from our Grandfather's farm in Suffolk. The river house was filled with the scents of baked lattice-top strawberry-rhubarb pies.

Lillian

Yesterday, after Sunday dinner, Frederick drove my husband back to Richmond. He returned this morning to take care of chores at the river house. After Hattie served lunch and the children went up for naps, I sat on the porch with my book. Even under the ceiling fan, it was stifling.

"Frederick, this heat is overbearing and I need to feel

34

some cool breezes. I would like you to take me out in the rowboat to that blueberry patch down Chocaway Creek."

"Yes ma'am, Missus Lillian. I'll load up your berry basket and the buckets," he answered.

"We will leave in half an hour. Hattie will take care of Mary Margaret and the boys," I said.

When the boat was ready, Frederick steadied it at the pier and offered me his hand. I settled onto a cushion on the center seat. He loosened the rope from the piling, stepped into the boat, and used one oar to push away from the dock. He began a smooth, evenly paced rowing motion. He dipped the oars into the surface of the khaki-colored water and pulled back to leave dips and ripples. I opened an old-fashioned, ruffled parasol that had been my grandmother's.

We glided upriver past the grasses lining the bank. When we turned left into the mouth of the creek, a great blue heron lifted from the cattail reeds and winged like a heavy plane just ahead of the boat bow.

"Missus Lillian," Frederick said, "There be some dark clouds behind. Maybe we don't go all the way up the crik."

"You know that's where the blueberry patch is. We will be fine. Anyway, the wind is blowing away from us," I said. "Look, there's an eagle's nest."

I pulled my opera glasses from the pocket of my sundress. "And there's the eagle on top of that old dead tree."

Frederick rested the oars on his knees so we could drift silently past the regal bird that surveyed the water and the marshes. Before we reached the narrow part of the creek, where it curved to pass under the bridge for the Route 17 highway, he turned the boat to a narrow beach on a small island that split the creek.

Someone had built a fishing shack on the knoll of the island. The weathered shack had bits of broken glass in the windows and loose-hinged shutters. Perhaps a fisherman had brought along a pail of fruit to eat. Brambles of blackberries and raspberries, blueberry bushes, and peach trees were scattered all around. The birds seemed to love this mecca.

I marked the date in my journal that the fruit was ripe and plentiful before the birds could scavenge the vines and trees.

While we gathered fruit, Frederick held onto one of the oars and looked out for snakes in the undergrowth that was lit by splashes of sunlight.

When the full pails were loaded into the front of the boat, I settled once again on the middle seat. Frederick pushed off into the center of the creek. As he rowed, the sky darkened. The wind bent the trees on the riverbank and turned up silver-sided leaves. The temperature dropped form 90 degrees to what felt like 30 degrees.

"I thinks we better turn back. There's lightnin' ahead," Frederick said as he slowed his rowing toward the river.

I bent over my lap, clutched my wide-brimmed hat and pulled the skirt of my sundress tight around my legs. Frederick turned the boat back toward the island and the shelter of the fishing shack and tied up to a large tree that had fallen along the bank.

"Missus Lillian," he said loudly over wind, "You take my hand. We'll go up to that cabin."

The wind pushed against us at hurricane force. Once inside, I cried as hail pelted through the windows. "I am freezing! I am scared! Do something, Frederick!"

As we stood in the center of the hut, Frederick pulled an old metal cot toward a wall away from the windows, shook out a moth-eaten blanket, and gently helped me lie down. Even after he covered me up, I shivered and my teeth chattered. Thunder shook the cabin and lightning lit up the trees in a strobe-like effect.

"Frederick. Please do something," I wailed.

He hesitated. "Missus Lillian, there's no way to make a fire. The only thing I might do is lie down there wit' you and try to warm you up."

"Well, then do that," I screamed as lightning and thunder collided all around us.

Frederick kneeled beside the cot, carefully turned me on my side, facing away from him, and wrapped his arms around my blanketed body to warm us both. My shivering gradually slowed to an occasional tremble. His face was so close to my ear that his breath warmed me like glowing embers in an open hearth. I turned over and my lips touched his in an almost accidental moment. He jerked his head back.

"Shush," I whispered. "I fear we will never leave here alive. And this is our final day on this earth."

I moved my pale hands to his dark cheeks. "I have never touched a Negro before. Your skin is as warm as bread from the oven."

I kissed him lightly, as if exploring a fleshy plum surface. It seemed like hours before the storm passed on upriver. The wind that blew through the broken windows left behind a mist of salt from the Chesapeake Bay that sprinkled a glaze on their skin.

Frederick rose from the cot and went outside empty water from the bottom of the boat with a pail. After I was settled on my bench, he gathered the oars he had stashed in the brush, and untied the boat.

Lillian: After the Storm

I was still shaken up by what happened now that Frederick was missing. This morning he rowed my husband out on the boat to check the crab pots. My husband was the only one to return. He insisted that there was no reason to call the police. "After all," he said, "he was only a servant." Then he looked out the window and said, "He jumped from the boat near the far shore and ran away."

I just don't know what the truth might be. Did my husband push Frederick off the boat? Did he drown? I had to write this all down in my journal, as though it was a dream I would soon forget.

The following month I drifted through clouds that darkened my soul. I uttered disconnected words to the bedroom walls, out the window to the hay fields, and across the surface of the broad river. I had sudden urges to run from the house, my children, and my life.

When my father came up from Suffolk at the end of that month, he found me trembling under a layer of bed covers one would usually only use on a cold winter night.

"Lillian, wake up, dear. Your husband asked me to come

check on you," he said. He laid his broad hand on my shoulder. This was the hand of a trusted father and revered physician.

"Lillian, I need you to wake up, honey. I am going to give you something to calm you down," he lifted my lids and shone a small penlight into my eyes. "I am going to take you someplace where you can rest."

He pulled a large syringe and medicine vial of a reddish-brown liquid from his worn, brown satchel. I remembered that he carried doses of the opiate laudanum when he made house calls. And now he had driven all this way to take care of me. When he gave me the shot in my arm, I cried out in pain, then became silent. He called out to the living room where Hattie was waiting.

"Hattie, would you get my daughter ready for the trip?" he said.

She came in so quietly I could barely hear her soft breathing. She gently pulled back the blankets and helped me sit up against the pillows. She slipped each of my arms into a long bathrobe and pulled my legs to the side of the bed. Then she put her wrinkled arms around me to lift me into the wheelchair father had brought with him. I heard muffled sobbing and felt quivering from her chest.

Father and Hattie placed me into the backseat of his car, laid me down, and covered me with a quilt. I started to feel strange, not sleepy, but numb from my face down through my toes.

It seemed we had driven for hours through the flat Tidewater and Piedmont regions. I must have dozed off, for I woke to feel the steep curves of the highway going over Afton Mountain and the Blue Ridge range.

We must be on Route 250 beyond Charlottesville. I shivered in a panic to think that my father was not taking me home to Richmond. Where were we going? I could not even whisper the words to ask. The medicine had numbed my voice.

The car finally stopped in front of the portico of a large, colonnaded building. Father came around to help me sit up in the backseat. Through the car window, I saw a manicured green lawn and beautiful terraced gardens that stretched gradually down the slope from the circular drive. This place reminded me of the Homestead in Hot Springs, where we would vacation as a family when I was young. But this eerie building was not that hotel.

Three men in white jackets walked down the broad steps. The more elderly looking man shook hands with my father. "Good morning, Dr. McCormick. How are you?" he said.

"Good morning, Dr. Dejarnette. I have brought my daughter for you to treat," my father responded in a somber voice.

The attendants were silent as they helped me into another wheelchair and rolled me down the sidewalk toward a lower-level entrance. I looked around, but my father was still talking with the doctor. He did not even say good-bye to me. I thought that perhaps he would be staying also.

I began to cry when I saw a sign that read Western State Hospital, but no tears came from my eyes. No tears ran down my cheeks. Inside the hallway, I heard whispers of the words "asylum" and "mental illness" and "lunatic." I sensed demons ravaging the patients in the rooms that we passed.

I thought I had slept for days when the nurse woke me for a meeting with the doctor. He asked how I was feeling.

I responded, "I am merely here during my pregnancy, and then I will be ready to go home."

"Mrs. Fitzpatrick, you are here in the hospital, not only because of your medical circumstances, but also for your mood swings and other abnormalities," he said.

When he lined up a row of prescription bottles with my name on the labels, I bolted up out of the chair. "I have never taken these medicines before. I do not understand."

"You will need to stay calm until your infant is born in the winter. Then you will need to be here at least six months after so that we can stabilize your mood swings," he answered in a monotone voice.

Over the weeks, my appetite plummeted, but my stomach grew larger. An IV pushed nutrients and fluids into my body. The doctor prescribed injections that the nurses administered every morning. I did not see or hold my body when it was born. A nurse told me in an unemotional voice that the baby had died.

Mary Margaret: 1955

The summer of 1935 had changed my life forever. I retreated into confused thoughts at home and at school. I had lost my childhood as if it the memories belonged to some other girl. Our family presented normalcy to friends and neighbors. We never talked about Frederick's disappearance. No one besides my father and grandfather, and perhaps Hattie, knew what really happened. My mother's sporadic trips to Western State masqueraded as vacations to visit her father's farm. Hattie raised my brothers and me through college and into adulthood.

The past twenty years I have tried to deduce from the final entries in Mother's diary what happened that summer. She had left her journal behind, hidden in the rafters of the river house when my grandfather took her off to the hospital the first time.

As far as I knew, she never made another entry when she came home to Richmond almost a year later. She was an empty shell, with only the slight echo of an infinite sea in her soul and a dark cavernous look in her eyes.

The funeral this week in the Cathedral of the Sacred Heart was elaborate and lengthy. As I listened to the eulogies, I realized I did not know this side of my father that his business colleagues described. At Hollywood Cemetery, my brothers stood on either of Mother to support her thin body. As our father's casket was lowered, I watched the gaze of my mother's eyes as they moved to the left toward the far side of the marble tombstones.

There stood a tall, gray-haired man with his head raised. His skin was dark as a Grecian urn with an age-worn, crackled surface. Frederick's brown eyes lifted to meet my mother's slight smile. A tall, young man with light brown skin, reddish-brown hair, and my mother's green eyes stood by his side.

Lucky

Jean Lancaster

(Honorable mention fiction, Virginia Writers Club 2014 Summer Shorts Writing Contest)

I have always believed that Aloysius Saint Luke, who was named for saints and nicknamed Lucky early in life, had nine or more lives. I concluded this despite the fact that he was not of the feline breed. Lucky has been my faithful companion for almost as long as the English literature dissertation of my midlife crisis transition has lingered on my vintage rolltop desk.

Lucky's loyalty has indeed been like the evangelist Luke's was to Paul in the early years as described in the New Testament. If Lucky could pray for me, he probably would howl up to Expeditus, a patron saint for perpetual students and others with unfinished projects.

I lived most of my adult life of procrastination in a sprawling house on the Rappahannock River that I inherited from my grandmother. It was there that I once witnessed this phenomenon of Lucky's persistent survival.

Hurricane Sandy was off the coast of Virginia. About an hour before the rains were expected, I stood out on my pier that extended into the river. I stubbed out my cigar, pulled my UVa baseball cap down tight, and snapped up my yellow slicker. As the winds pounded, I worked the ropes into bowline knots to secure my fishing boat.

Lucky and I seemed to be directly in the face of an approaching tempest that everyone called the Superstorm. Spinning winds uprooted the river's water into wave-like surges. Thunder bellowed and lightning sizzled.

Lucky was hunkered down under the oldest tree around, its gnarled branches bending and cracking. A boom and a howling shriek erupted. As Lucky raced away, I saw a zigzag pattern carved in his chocolate-brown fur, starting at his blue collar and zipping all the way down to his pelvis.

I finally found Lucky seven days later, asleep and

snoring, in the shade of the swing on my front porch. His fur was growing back, but he still smelled of singed flesh. He greeted me seemingly without any memory of the lightning strike. I thought then that, no matter how badly you are burned, you always returned to those who loved you.

Years earlier, when Lucky was a two-year-old pup, we stayed for a week in a friend's cabin on the Bullpasture River in western Virginia. Toward the end of the week, we crossed the river and hiked to Marshall's Cave midway up Bullpasture Mountain. Returning from our caving trek, I tottered along the swinging rope bridge that goes from the mountainside trail back over to a campground.

Halfway across and ahead of me, Lucky spotted a rainbow trout as it leapt up and spun above the torrential water. Lucky made a dashing leap between the support ropes and dove headfirst into the river. The rounded rocks below knocked him out cold.

I raced the rest of the way across the bridge and jumped into the rushing water. I wrapped my arms around Lucky and laid him out on the primeval rock ledge while the river cascaded around us. I put my ear to his chest trying to hear his heartbeat.

As I cried and soothed his soft brown forehead, he opened one eye and sneezed out white river foam. Then he licked my face with sloppy drool to relay his gratitude and acknowledge my courage.

Surely there was much more to Lucky's devotion to me than my life-saving efforts. "Hounds follow those who feed them," Count Otto Bismarck was quoted as saying. Lucky was indeed grateful for our feeding routine.

I believe that his dedication was the reason he always wanted to go along with me wherever I went. The few times he did not ride on the passenger seat of my rusted '57 Chevy pickup, he waited in an unwavering sprawl on the porch. He was not a dog to run away the minute I was out of sight. When I pulled back in the driveway, allegiance sparkled in his eyes like fireworks on the Fourth of July.

The sparkle disappeared from Lucky's eyes one time; and I thought I was going to lose him. We started the morning at our favorite fishing spot. The azure pond seemed to float on the surface of the marsh. I cast out my line for the mammoth largemouth bass that lurked in the water.

Lucky waded through the low water, followed his Labrador retriever ancestral memories, and nosed around for unsuspecting ducks. From the corner of my eye, I spotted the glide of the four-foot-long water moccasin. Before I could even blink, the toxic fangs struck Lucky's barreled chest.

I sloshed through and picked up my already lethargic dog. By the time I laid him on the front seat of the truck, his chest was swollen into a pregnant mass. I sped to the vet's office where he received the antivenom serum. My arms cradled him throughout the night until, as if it was a normal day, he licked my chin when he woke from the anesthesia.

Other, less terrifying episodes have added to the count of Lucky's numerous incarnations. There was the time Lucky was the unfortunate cleanup crew after a cookout I had with friends. He reclined on the deck during our party late into the night, just waiting for his opportunity to be one of the guys.

The next morning I found evidence that he had ripped open a package of sodium-laden hot dogs and downed almost a dozen. He had knocked over unfinished, open beers to lap up the warm liquid. I found him in a stupor on one of the lounge chairs. As the Irish satirist Jonathan Swift said, "Every dog must have his day."

These days, Lucky takes medication for an aging-related ailment. Twice a day I coax him into taking the large white capsules by hiding each one in a spoonful of vanilla ice cream. One night, instead of licking the sweet treat, he swallowed the whole spoon. He fortunately hurled it back up, instead of waiting for the spoon to pass through his stomach and intestines.

These episodes of defying death and overcoming severe injury have accompanied Lucky and me through life and into manhood. I am officially a senior citizen and Lucky is fifteen, seventy-three in man years. He is aging noticeably. He struggles to rise up onto all fours. He is deaf and looks at me with dull eyes when I talk to him. His appetite is gone, even for his favorite bacon cooked to a crisp in the cast-iron skillet. Lucky never whimpers or whines to complain about his aches and pains. Vincent van Gogh, suffering from ill health, wrote in one of his letters, "To suffer without complaint is the only lesson we have to learn in this life."

Lucky and I have lived through the fragility of life, which he tested to dramatic limits. According to novelist Robert Louis Stevenson, "You think those dogs will not be in heaven? I tell you they will be there long before any of us." Although, I dread the day Lucky goes to the life beyond, I feel that he will enter the pearly gates before me and wait with his tail wagging and his faithful eyes shining bright.

Nun Run

Elaine Ruggieri

(First place fiction, Blue Ridge Writers VWC, 2014)

My Aunt Carmen liked bars. I found out when she asked if I'd go with her to drive two nuns to a convent near Philadelphia. Her kids were in school, and I was on college break. I hesitated. Nuns!

"Won't take long. We'll drop them off and then we'll go to a nice bar I know," she said. Carmen's knowing a Philadelphia bar sounded as strange to me as transporting nuns.

Will I have to pray, I wondered, thinking of the rosary, bead by bead. Nuns and men with round white collars intimidated me. I didn't go to Catholic school, but I still feared the parish priests and the nuns, especially the good sisters of St. Joseph. They drilled the catechism into us public school kids during our required after-school classes two days a week, and they taught us more lessons after mass on Sunday. Sister Ann Marie would often ask why I didn't go to Catholic school, and didn't I want to be a nun like her? How does an eight-year-old tomboy honestly answer? My mother doesn't want us hit with a ruler and I like playing baseball with the boys?

I hadn't talked to a sister of the cloth since my confirmation ceremony, another nun-dreading event when Reverend Mother clicked her cricket to make us genuflect in unison. We had to impress the bishop on cue and answer catechism questions as His Excellency walked among us. We trembled in our pews, suppressing acid reflux, and praying, "Spare me, Lord, and I'll never lie again." The man in the miter came close but interrogated the kid next to me. That marked the end of my instruction classes. Once confirmed, I forgot all about catechism and Sister Ann Marie.

My aunt Carmen didn't go to church either except for family ceremonies like weddings and funerals, but she sent her kids to the parochial school with bursting collection envelopes, so I guess she was pardoned. Carmen was also my godmother, sworn to look after my Catholic upbringing. I couldn't blame my religious lapse on her neglect of duties, or worse, expose hers to the church.

"OK, I'll go with you," I answered without enthusiasm. "But where do I have to sit?" I was dreading the backseat next to some pinched-faced nun who would stare at my too-casual clothes, painted fingernails, and orange lipstick.

Carmen laughed and told me, "They" always sit in the back and are usually silent. "If they had asked me earlier, I could have gotten us tickets to see the Phils game."

Carmen was a big baseball fan and followed the Philadelphia and New York teams of the early 1950s—the Athletics, Phillies, Yankees, Dodgers, and Giants. During the season, one of these teams was usually on her black-and-white TV. As she watched, she smoked Camels and ate Baby Ruths.

"Instead, we'll stop at Guido's Bar. The best Philly steaks and pizza in the city! Not to mention the Manhattans. And, the Phillies might be on television. Be ready around one. Can't be late."

She sensed my uneasiness. "Take a book and say you have to read it for college. They'll leave you alone." Good advice, but the book I had to finish was *Madame Bovary*. Convent dropout, French adulterer, defective mother, Church scofflaw. Suppose they asked what I was studying. I couldn't lie. I promised the Lord. However, I could honestly say it was assigned reading and not my personal choice.

"Relax," said Carmen. "They read the Bible, don't they? Where do you think all that adultery stuff started?"

"Can we talk? To each other, I mean. Just you and me?"

"No vows of silence, but they'll be listening, honey. Better you read, I drive, and they pray."

I was dreading their questions. Did I go to church every Sunday? Did I go to confession? Are you a member of the Newman Club? "Yes" to only the last one, but they wouldn't like why. I joined the Newman Club because that's where so many good-looking Penn State football players went on Thursday nights.

"What's your favorite at Guido's?" I asked. The thought of a good Philly cheese steak sandwich briefly calmed my anxiety.

"All delicious, and the Manhattans are the best," said Carmen. "Guido's is the fun part of the trip. You'll see." She looked at me. "Relax, Nina. And, be grateful for all the blessings we'll get from the holy sisters. Can't hurt."

Carmen was my father's sister. He never went to church much either, often disparaged priests, but contributed money for special collections. I overheard him say once to Carmen, "Sure, I don't go to communion. Who knows where that priest's hand's been?" My mother, a faithful, sinless Catholic, didn't actually lie when the parish priest paid a yearly visit and asked when my father last received holy communion, but she'd shake her head to mean "who knows, or yes, he's going straight to hell, Father." My brother, like most young men his age, hardly ever talked about religion and went to mass only by habit.

Carmen was prompt. We parked before the gray-stone convent beside the gray-stone church beside the gray-stone school. A fortress! As a kid, I wondered what the nuns did in there. I would get as far as the front door, delivering an envelope with cash or a cake for a bake sale, and happy to be dismissed with, "We'll thank your mother in our prayers. God bless her." I'd turn and run home.

We walked to the front door that immediately opened, and, holy hell! There was my old instructor, Sister Ann Marie, showing a few wrinkles, made deeper by her wimple, with a nun I didn't recognize. Carmen introduced me. Sister Ann Marie nodded, fake-smiled, and introduced the Reverend Mother as she eyed me. I pinched my lips to hide the orange glow.

"I remember you, Nina. You and your brother came for catechism. I suppose you're in college now?"

"Yes, Sister. Penn State. My brother too." She looked as if she could still flatten a student with one swing of a ruler. I never saw her do it, but I heard the tales. "Let me carry your bag, Sister." She handed me hers and Reverend Mother's, identical valises in black leather, with crosses embossed on the sides. They didn't weigh much. The nuns didn't own much.

"How long will you be staying?" asked Carmen.

47

"Just overnight, Mrs. Pinto. We have a ride back with Father Dolan. Bless you for helping us today."

"No trouble, Reverend Mother. Happy to do it. And I get to spend some time with my favorite niece." I knew all five of her nieces were her favorite, but I appreciated the compliment with Sister Ann Marie in earshot. I smiled at Aunt Carmen's support.

They settled in the back, valises on the floor, and we drove off. Carmen's husband always had the newest car in the family, usually a Plymouth. It was a treat to ride in luxury and sit on shiny seats. Our 1947 Chevy had dents, rusted fenders, bald tires, and frayed upholstery.

The Reverend Mother noticed. "This is such a lovely car, Mrs. Pinto."

"Yes, so comfortable," said Sister Ann Marie. Then, she asked, "Do you like the book, Nina?" Carmen shot me a glance.

Turning slowly toward the back, I said, "Just something I have to finish. Assigned reading. I'm not very far." I knew that didn't answer her question and feared she would persist.

"It's *Madame Bovary*, isn't it? I saw it when I got in." Why didn't I cover it up? Carmen was smiling like the Cheshire cat.

"Yes, Sister." I said and turned toward the front, hoping that would end it.

"I had to read it too. Long time ago. Emma is a woman who does bad things and then pays for her sins." She didn't have to add, "And let that be a lesson to you, young lady."

I wanted to say I just couldn't *wait* for Emma to do "bad" things, but I turned a page instead and feigned interest in Emma's boredom with country living in nineteenth-century France.

"Speaking of reading, we have some to do, don't we, Sister?" Reverend Mother said as she pulled a notebook out of her valise. "Unfortunately, this is not a pleasure trip."

"Yes, Reverend Mother," said Sister Ann Marie in a deferential tone. She quickly retrieved her notebook and opened it.

Carmen, looking straight ahead, gave me a quick thumbs-up down by her knees.

For the rest of the hour-long drive, we were silent except when Carmen asked if anyone wanted a mint. There were no takers, but Reverend Mother said, "We don't want to spoil our appetites. The sisters at Villanova have prepared refreshments just for us. They insisted they treat you."

My heart sank. No Guido's? I looked at Carmen. "That's so nice of them, Reverend Mother, but I really should turn right around and head home to my husband and kids," Carmen said.

"Oh, they would be so disappointed, Mrs. Pinto. We won't keep you long, and they are so looking forward to your visit. We don't entertain often."

"Well, I guess we can. Just not for long."

I wondered what the refreshments would be. Tea or coffee would be nice. I was getting drowsy.

"Park right in front, Mrs. Pinto," said Reverend Mother. "It's usually saved for visiting priests, but you are special today."

Carmen stopped the car, and we both hopped out to open the doors for our backseat passengers. I took their bags again, and we walked toward the front door of the gray-stone Villanova convent. Before we could knock, two nuns opened the door and greeted us, thanking the Lord for our safe journey. Reverend Mother handled the introductions. She said Carmen was a dedicated, loyal member of their parish and I was her niece Nina on a holiday from Penn State.

"Welcome, welcome. Please come in. We've prepared some refreshments for you so you won't drive home on empty stomachs," said Sister Margaret Agnes. There goes Guido's now, I thought.

We were shown into a small sitting room, plainly decorated, with a wooden crucifix over the mantel, brightly colored pictures of Jesus and the Madonna on the walls, and a statue of St. Joseph placed in a bay window. I noticed the afternoon sunlight glinting off his head like a halo.

"Isn't that just the perfect spot for our patron saint, Nina?" Sister Ann Marie asked.

"Yes, Sister, it is." I then looked at the coffee table and the prepared refreshments that would tide us over—a tray with six Nabisco Mallomar cookies, those chocolate covered marshmallows with graham cracker bottoms, and six glasses filled with an amber liquid.

After a short grace, they passed the cookies and drinks. "Oh, what a treat!" said Carmen. "These are my favorites." She took a napkin from the tray and placed one cookie on it. I followed her lead, and said, "Thank you, Sister. I am a little thirsty." I hoped Sister Margaret Agnes didn't see the tremor as I held the glass.

"We thought and thought about what to prepare for you, and Sister Catherine Clare suggested that cookies and ginger ale would be perfect," said Sister Margaret Agnes.

"And, she was right," said Carmen. I envied her ease in talking to nuns. I could hardly swallow. I nodded and nibbled at the cookie, pretending it was indeed stemming my hunger. To avoid looking at Sister Ann Marie, I concentrated on the diminishing Mallomar.

After a short conversation on how I liked college, what my major was, and how Carmen's children were doing in school, Carmen rose and said she was sorry to eat and run, but she knew they had things to do and we had to get on the road. After many thanks from the sisters to us and us to them, the nuns, with their black skirts swishing and their rosary beads rattling, walked us quickly to the door and recited their many blessings for a safe trip.

"Finish the book," whispered Sister Ann Marie. She looked directly at me and clasped my hand with her bony, but strong fingers.

"I will. I have to, Sister," I said with a little smile.

"I pitied poor Emma. I felt sorry for her at the end. You'll see. May God bless you, Nina." As we walked to the car, I turned, thinking I might wave good-bye to Sister Ann Marie, but the nuns were making the sign of the cross before walking inside.

We were silent until Carmen pulled away. I was feeling ungrateful after their hospitality and prayers for our safety, and a little ashamed of my childhood judgment of Sister Ann Marie. "May God bless you, Nina," she had said with such warmth. I didn't even say "thank-you."

"Does this mean no Guido's?" I asked.

"Are you kidding? After that sugar high, I need a drink and some solid food," said Carmen, who started to giggle.

"We shouldn't laugh," said Carmen, still doing it. "They had to pay for those treats with their own money and they don't have a lot. Six cookies and six drinks. What a feast!" It tickled her. "And, now I can smoke!"

Guido's was one of those corner bars at the end of a block of brick row houses in a mixed neighborhood of residences, small grocery stores, restaurants, and bars. In these local taverns, the owner usually tended bar and his wife or another family member cooked.

"Carmen! *Benvenuto!* Where you been?" Guido greeted us. Carmen had told me Guido was old Mrs. Regalli's son and his in-laws owned this bar for years. Now he and his wife were running it, and had changed the name from Gianni's to Guido's. In that neighborhood, the name change needed no explanation.

"Just did another nun run, Guido. No game today but got some points in heaven. This is my niece Nina."

"*Bene, bene!* So, you can see the Phillies here. Now what do you beautiful ladies want?" He stared at me. "Nina, are you of age? You know, I have to ask." He hunched his shoulders, showing he didn't make the rules.

"Twenty-one," I said and showed him my driver's license, even though Carmen was nodding that I was OK. A priest once gave me severe penance for lying with fake IDs, but I continued the sin until I hit the legal age.

"We'll split a medium pepperoni pizza and a cheese steak each. And, Guido, I want a large sausage pizza and three sandwiches to go. My family will be waiting at the door," said Carmen.

"And, now? A Manhattan for Carmen, right? Nina?"

"A draft," I said, wondering how the beer would mix with the ginger ale and Mallomars.

"No, give her a Manhattan too," said Carmen. "Guido mixes a good one, and I'll drink yours if you don't like it. You college kids drink too much beer."

Carmen was studying the television, small by today's models. The Phils were beating the Giants. "They should win this game," she said.

"Yeah, but they could still screw up," said Guido. "Just like the other day. I'm sticking with the Yankees."

"Can't go wrong there," said Carmen. I was a Yankees fan too, but didn't follow baseball the way Carmen and my brother did. I left Carmen and Guido talking about Joe DiMaggio and went to the restroom.

Seated at the bar were three men also staring at the game, drinking beer, smoking. An older couple sat at a table eating pizza and drinking the house red. They all smiled as I walked by. Immediate acceptance was nice. The smell of sausage, tomato sauce, and cheese came from the kitchen. A radio was playing Puccini arias, just audible above the baseball game. I liked this place. Carmen did know bars.

"Isn't this nice? I love bar stools. Nothing better than a friendly bar in the afternoon. Good drinks, good food. I like to treat myself every time I'm in Philly," said Carmen.

She was sipping her Manhattan between drags of a cigarette. "How's yours?"

"Stronger than I'm used to," I said. "Lot stronger than ginger ale." We both laughed.

"Do you think we left too soon? Was it rude?"

"No. Nuns have work to do, prayers to say, papers to grade. I never stay too long. The six cookies and six glasses were a message. No seconds and no time. Maybe, no money too. Just sip the Manhattan and you'll enjoy it more."

"Did you notice how Reverend Mother changed the subject of Madame Bovary in the car? She saved me."

"She's not *Reverend Mother* for nothing, you know. She was afraid Sister Ann Marie might discuss Madame Bovary's sinful ways and put you on the spot. You don't antagonize your benefactors or their relatives."

The pizza and the sandwiches arrived. "*Buon appetito!*" said Guido.

"Smells so good!" said Carmen. "I'll tell your mother I stopped in. She raves about this place all the time."

"What can I say? She's my mother!" said Guido, smiling. "Want another Manhattan? The couple over there's treating. Anniversary."

"How can I refuse?" She looked at the couple, raised her glass, and drained the rest of her drink. They returned the toast, saying, "*Salute.*"

"Mine's not sitting too well with the Mallomars."

"You drive home, Nina. These Manhattans are loaded, and I couldn't turn down the freebie. Wouldn't be nice."

On the ride back with the savory smell of the to-go pizza and sandwiches wafting from the backseat, I drove while Carmen slumped. I thought about Sister Ann Marie. What made her become a nun? Where did she read *Madame Bovary*? How old was she when she taught us catechism? What did she do before taking the vows?

"Carmen, did you notice how Sister Ann Marie kept staring at me? I felt so guilty. Like I was Madame Bovary or something!"

"Oh, don't dwell on it. She said she felt sorry for her."

"Didn't expect that. By the way, did Mom suggest that you take me today?"

"No. Why?"

"Well, I've been avoiding religion like a drunk uncle except for going to the Newman Club. And, a friend of mine told Mom on Parents Weekend that she knocked on my door every Sunday to go to mass, but I slept in. Nuns and priests still make me feel so sinful, you know."

"They're supposed to. Look, your mother warned me you might say no. That's all. I just wanted your company. And, kill the guilt. You can't be Madame Bovary. You're not even married."

I was silent, thinking how routine it used to be to study the catechism, go to mass, get smudged on Ash Wednesday, give up watermelon for Lent, go to confession with made-up sins; observe all the Catholic rituals. I didn't question my faith then. I just resented the time it took. I looked over at Carmen, still slumped with eyes closed. I hoped she didn't have two Manhattans every time at Guido's.

"Going to mass or not is your business. You're old enough. Oh, I know they tell us it's a mortal sin to miss mass, but to me mortal sin means sin committed by mere mortals, us sinful souls! Not mortal as in 'fatal' and 'straight to the Devil with you!' As I said, what would they do without us sinners?" said Carmen.

"Spoken like a true godmother," I said, making Carmen laugh. "I never knew you liked bars. And, Manhattans."

"We grew up right after Prohibition ended. Your uncle and I would go to bars on Saturday nights. Drink, dance, smoke, play poker. Fun! Not Sister Anne Marie's kind, but most of us would get up and go to mass the next day. Maybe a little hung over," she said, looking at me now with a wink and a smile.

When we arrived in front of my house, I leaned over to give her a hug and to thank her. "You all right to drive home?"

"Oh, sure. That solid Italian food soaked up all that alcohol. If only that couple hadn't bought a round. Made me sleepy."

"And the nuns?" she asked.

"Umm. Surprising. Scary, but nice. Real nice. Never thought I'd see Sister Ann Marie again. She still got me with those stares."

"Forget the guilts, Nina. Or, go to confession. You'll feel better. And, remember, she gave you a personal blessing."

"Yeah, I know. Can't hurt. Right?"

Carmen saw my mother on the porch, and yelled to her, "Hey, I think Nina wants to go to church with you on Sunday." She laughed, blew the horn, and drove away.

JFK, Daddy, and Me

Deborah M. Prum

(Second place fiction, Blue Ridge Writers VWC, 2014)

Late at night, in my small bedroom, by the soft yellow beam of my father's flashlight, I used a blue ballpoint pen to scratch out a story about a band of orphans who were stranded on a gorgeous tropical island—a place very different from New Britain, Connecticut, the grimy factory town where I lived.

Meanwhile, Ma and Daddy screamed at each other in the kitchen. They'd fought before. Plenty of times. But never this bad. For several weeks, my father had been coming home late from his dispatcher job at the police station.

"Where you been, Mick? Four hours past supper." Ma banged a pot.

"Ha! But I'm damn early for breakfast." Daddy slurred his words.

"You're dead drunk. What's that smell? You stink."

"I stink? This apartment stinks of garlic. Reeks." I heard Daddy fall onto the chrome kitchen chair, knocking it over. "Marrying into an Italian family—I'm cursed with a lifetime of garlic." My father seemed to be giggling.

"Beer and smoke." Ma paused. "And her cheap perfume. You can't fool me. I can smell that, too. A stench like disinfectant."

My father never drank that much, sometimes one beer on Friday night. After that, he'd sing some Irish tunes—crazy songs—one about a girl so skinny she slipped down the bathtub drain. Once, he sang that Elvis hound dog song and wound up howling, which made even my grumpy mother laugh a little.

A scrape and a bump, maybe Ma picked up the chair and then set it against the Formica table. I couldn't tell. I prayed that God would stop the fighting. I waited, hopeful for a quick answer. But no, if anything, my parents shouted louder, hurling violent words at each other.

Did other families fight like this? Not on *Leave It to Beaver* or *My Three Sons*. Every show, those people disagreed about something—but no screaming and yelling. And, by the end, always lots of smiles and jokey talk.

I tried to go back to writing my story. I forced myself to picture a starry night and happy orphans—children not tortured by fighting parents—those lucky kids, stirring a delicious stew over a warm campfire. Not one word came to mind. So, instead, in the margin of the paper, I sketched a picture of myself: curly black hair, green eyes behind blue-rimmed glasses. I tried to make my face look happy, but the mouth came out all wrong. Above my head, I drew the ragged leaves of a palm tree. That wasn't quite right, either. I looked so very tiny.

More words. This time Ma saying that despite all his promises, all his big talk, they were getting nowhere, still stuck in a rat hole.

Rat hole? At least that's what I thought I'd heard. My mother tended to exaggerate. My room had a comfortable bed, red plaid café curtains, a wooden rolltop desk, a narrow three-legged bureau, a pile of books forming the fourth leg. Not much, but not a rat hole either. My mother complained—to Nonnie, my grandmother and to all our friends—how we were going nowhere fast, how she'd had bigger ideas for her life. Once I overheard my parents talking about sending my mother to accounting school. My father said something like, "Angie, I'll work my way up in the department, you'll see. The minute I do, it's off to school for you."

I wished someone would show up at the apartment door—specifically an angel. An angel who behaved like a tooth fairy; someone who could wave a sparkly wand and undo the mess. Presto! My father would come home on time and sober, with an arm full of flowers for Ma. He'd give her a big smooch. And Ma, well, she'd smile then hug him hard.

But no angel, no tooth fairy, no nobody. I buried my head under the pillow. Didn't matter. I could still hear them.

"You got a woman, don't you? Go stay with her." Ma's voice sounded raw. I couldn't stand it. I hit my head with the flashlight, little thunks, but hard enough to hurt. Somehow, that pain helped me get through the ache of listening to my parents shred each other.

"A woman? A woman!" Daddy's voice battered the air. He started laughing, laughing and sobbing at the same time. "Maybe I will leave. And I'm taking the money. I earned it. Every bloody dime."

My parents tried to put aside a little cash each month, hoping to buy a tract house in Hazardville, tiny and square, only two bedrooms but with a bit of grass out front. "Anywhere away from the tenements." Ma would say. Nonnie owned the building we lived in. Both Ma and Daddy wanted to get out from under her thumb. But every month, they had to dip into the savings—a flat tire on the Oldsmobile, new uniform pants for Daddy, fillings for my teeth.

More yelling. I couldn't make out the words. Why didn't God make them stop? Maybe I should pray to a saint. Was there a Patron Saint of Fighting Parents? I never paid attention in catechism. Then again, maybe God gave me these arguing parents to punish me for being such a bad Catholic.

A door slammed. Their bedroom door? Pounding. Ma screaming, "No . . . Mick . . . stop."

I jumped out of bed, throwing covers aside, rushing into the kitchen. I saw them, kneeling by the stove, struggling over the small metal box where they kept their money. They looked like two children fighting on the playground, his head of sweaty red curls up against her wavy black hair. But they weren't children; they were my parents. They were supposed to be adults.

All the yelling must have wakened my grandmother, who lived in the apartment above, because the next thing I knew, Nonnie, who was as wide as she was tall, burst through the door with such force the doorknob left a huge dent in the wall.

Nonnie tackled my father and dragged him out onto the porch, bumping his head hard against the jamb. I've wondered if my grandmother could have overpowered him had he been sober. Probably. Probably she could have.

Nonnie gave my father one final shove. "You go now. Come back when not drunk." Daddy stumbled down the stairs, taking two at a time. Then Nonnie turned to me, saying, "Jemma, go to bed."

The next two nights I kept watch for my father, staring out the window by my bed, hoping I'd see the light on at his workshop behind our tenement. Usually, after working a day shift, my father would gobble down dinner and then head down to the shop, repairing radios, toasters, lawn mowers, whatever the neighbors brought—although they'd been bringing less and less.

But my father never showed. No call. No nothing. Ma said she didn't care, good riddance to bad rubbish, but I heard her crying at night.

A dull ache filled my chest. Each morning, I considered skipping school, heading to the station downtown, seeing if I could talk to my father. I knew exactly which bus to take there. But Ma had never let me ride the bus on my own, saying eleven was a little too young for that.

Even if I did go, I wondered if my father would hate for me to barge in at his job. He never once had brought me inside the station. Maybe he felt ashamed that he only answered phones or maybe he wanted to protect me from all the sadness. I don't know.

I did consider calling him. Almost dialed him several times. I knew the emergency number, but I worried about my mother catching me. The phone sat dead center on the kitchen counter. I'd never get away with it.

Bone-tired and heartsick, I dragged myself through one last day of school before the weekend. I had gym seventh period on Fridays and could play outside. Thank God for that, but to be honest, I was furious with God. I pictured him in the left-hand corner of the universe, standing with his back to me.

We kids bundled into our winter jackets and braced ourselves against a brisk November wind. As we filed out onto the schoolyard, Mr. Sweeney, the P.E. teacher, told us to line up for alley soccer. Each child sprinted toward a chalked-off section of the asphalt court. No one dared disobey him. He'd gotten injured in the Korean War and came back a hero. My father said the man acted a little off, a little strange, and maybe it wasn't such a good idea for him to be around kids. But I didn't think he was so bad. Unless the students misbehaved, Mr. Sweeney hardly paid attention to any of them, spending most of every gym class with a mint-green transistor radio glued to his ear.

Within a minute of Mr. Sweeney putting the ball in play, I got hold of it and started dribbling down the alley toward the goal. But a boy named Pete tripped me as I tried to make the shot. My bare knees skidded on the pavement. Worse yet, I missed the goal. Within seconds, Pete had kicked the ball clear toward the other side. Being trapped in a dress and patent leather shoes didn't help my playing ability. I wished I could wear pants and Keds to school.

Blood dripped down both my knees. I glared at Pete as I sat next to my teacher on the sidelines. Mr. Sweeney barely looked at me or my knees. Scraped knees probably didn't measure up to the injuries he had seen in the war.

I checked the dial on Mr. Sweeney's watch. One-thirty. Nonnie and Ma would be looking at *As the World Turns*. Since I could remember, nothing got in the way of them watching that soap opera. My father once said Nonnie would probably come back from the dead every afternoon just to keep up with the story.

A few minutes later, just as a child made a goal, Mr. Sweeney yelled, "Holy Mother of God!" This made no sense. He never cared about who won the games. I saw him hold out the radio in front of him, looking at it as if it were dripping with poison. Then, covering his face, he put the radio back to his ear.

Mr. Sweeney kept shaking his head. At last, he said, "Everyone go inside. Our president has been shot."

The principal sent all us kids straight home. I arrived to an empty apartment. When I went upstairs to my grandmother's, I found half the people from our tenement squished into Nonnie's parlor, watching Walter Cronkite. In our block, no one but Nonnie owned a television.

Sitting on the floor, I could barely see the screen, but I noticed that the newsman didn't have his jacket on. Strange. Mr. Cronkite always wore a suit jacket on television. He also kept taking his glasses off and repeating himself, about how there were three shots and maybe President Kennedy was dead, but maybe not.

Another reporter, one in Texas, was talking about a man who killed a cop. I didn't understand. Wasn't it the president who got shot?

Mrs. Domkowski, Mrs. Kaufmann, and Mrs. Perez all squeezed on the same sofa together, which was something. Most days these women squabbled about parking spaces, garbage cans, noisy kids, you name it. None of them spoke English well, which also didn't help. Daddy said that those people stepped off the boat and right into Nonnie's apartment building. Of course, after that they headed to the factories to work. Nonnie's tenement was not far from Stanley Tool and Fafnir Bearing. Everybody was welcome at the factories: long hours, low pay, and no English-speaking skills necessary.

Mrs. Perez ran her rosary beads through her fingers, one by one. Click, mumble, click, mumble. A cigarette dangled from Mr. Assaryan's mouth, the ashes fluttering down to the carpet. I wondered who was running his store on the corner and why Nonnie wasn't getting him an ashtray.

Then, just after 2:30, Mr. Cronkite announced that John F. Kennedy had died. Was he wiping tears from his eyes? I had never seen a newsman cry on TV.

The set stayed on all day and into the evening. Some people came and went, but most just stayed. Folks left food on the kitchen table—provolone cheese, salami, bread, olives, empanadas, chicken cutlets, stuffed cabbage, angel wings dusted with sugar. The neighbors picked at the food but didn't eat as much as you'd have thought. All day Saturday went the same way, everyone staring at the sad scenes on the screen. When the Rutgers college boys sang a requiem with the Philadelphia Orchestra playing behind them, even Mrs. Kaufmann cried. And that was something. She was a hard one. Never a smile or nice word. Ma said the woman survived a war camp and still had a number tattooed on her arm.

Every time the back door opened, I jumped up, hoping it'd be my father. But no daddy and no word from or about him. I felt bad about John Kennedy—he was young, handsome, and Catholic. A Catholic man in the presidency. Our whole church celebrated back on election night. Yes, I was sad about JFK, but

I remember feeling guilty that I was way sadder about my father being gone.

On Sunday morning, no neighbors showed up. Each family went to their own church, not Mrs. Kaufmann, of course. The priest at my church read a statement from Pope Paul. The pope said he was profoundly saddened. I felt profoundly saddened, too, by every damn thing. I could have thrown a chair through a stained glass window I felt so sad. I wondered if God felt sad too, or if he cared at all.

People wept and blew their noses and wept again. This reminded me of my Grandpa Padric's funeral, years ago. Oh how I wished I could be sitting on that wooden pew, snuggled under my father's arm. But my father was nowhere to be seen. I knew it was a sin for him to miss mass. That much I remembered from catechism. I wondered if God planned to send my father to hell.

Back home after church, my family ate our usual Sunday lunch—a light chicken soup with orzo, roasted chicken and potatoes, spaghetti and meatballs, always followed by a cake covered in whipped cream and soaked in rum. This day, though, we didn't gather at Nonnie's dark wooden table and we didn't quite make it to dessert.

We sat in the parlor, balancing plates in our laps, staring at the television. At first the screen showed President Kennedy's coffin traveling down Pennsylvania Avenue. But then, the picture changed to Oswald being taken out of the Dallas jail. I didn't know where he was going. But as Oswald came out into the parking area, in the lower right corner of the screen, I saw a man's back, then heard a shot. Lee Oswald gasped and fell to the side. Then the screen filled with scuffling bodies, pushing down the shooter.

I jumped to my feet, sending the plate of pasta and meatballs to the floor. No one seemed to care about the mess. A stretcher carried Oswald away. Not much later, a newsman announced that Oswald was dead. The neighbors must have heard the news on their radios. Within minutes, Nonnie's parlor filled to overflowing.

The shooting at the police station terrified me. My father worked at a police station. Was he safe? I went downstairs to our apartment, to my room, and crawled under the covers. I pushed away my fears about my father and the police station. Instead, I tried to picture the day last summer when my father taught me how to ride a two-wheeler. He ran by my side for hours, red-faced and breathless, making jokes the whole time: *If Ireland sank into the sea, which county would never go down? Cork, of course.*

At the end of the afternoon, my father and I lay with our backs against the small grassy hillside behind the school, discovering fantastic stories in the clouds overhead. I kept those images in mind as I fell into a deep sleep.

No school that Monday. All morning we watched famous people arrive for the funeral—Prince Philip, General de Gaulle, Haile Selassie. As the television showed the mass given at St. Matthew's Cathedral, I noticed my mother crossing herself with the parishioners on screen.

At the end of the mass, as little Caroline left the church, the cardinal leaned down and kissed her on the cheek. Big tears rolled down Nonnie's cheeks. I realized I'd never seen my grandmother cry.

As the pallbearers lifted the casket, John-John fidgeted at his mother's side. I pitied the child, losing his father so young. Jacqueline Kennedy whispered to him and took a paper from the boy's hand. Then John-John saluted his father. The picture shook; maybe the cameraman was crying, too?

I could not hold back my own tears. I ran down the wooden porch steps and sat down on the cement stoop at the bottom. I knew I had to talk with my father, to see if he was all right, to try to make him come home. Would the buses be running today? I didn't know. If I wanted to take the bus, I'd have to go inside and steal the fare. Too big a risk. I decided to walk to the station. Ma and Nonnie wouldn't miss me. Not today as they watched the funeral.

So, I headed downtown, trudging into the bitter wind, getting lost once, asking directions twice, but finally arriving. I paused in front of the heavy wooden door, frightened to go in. Through the large side window, I could see my father sitting by a counter, talking on the phone. Would he be angry?

My father jumped up from his chair and scooped me into his arms, holding me close for a long time. I burrowed into his hug, never wanting to leave.

"Where have you been? You're mother just called. She's worried sick. Go ahead. Sit down now. I've got to let her know you're OK." He pointed to a wooden bench and then dialed my mother.

My father turned his back to me, cradling the receiver, talking quietly into the phone. I couldn't hear the words, only the tone of the words, quiet reassuring murmurs. He spoke much longer than it would take to convey a simple message. I dared to hope.

After my father hung up, another cop came by. "Mick, go on. Your shift is almost over anyway. I'll cover for you."

My father grabbed his hat, scarf, and jacket from a locker and we left out the back door.

Once outside, my father asked, "Jemma, how in the world did you get here?"

"Walked." I lowered my head, bracing for a lecture.

Instead, my father grabbed my shoulders. "Good lord, girl. Five miles?"

"I had to see if you were all right."

My father pulled me into another hug. He shook a bit as he spoke. "All right. Yes, I'm all right. But sad and very ashamed."

The wind picked up. Daddy wrapped his scarf around my neck. "Buses aren't running. Let's get going. Your mother will be waiting."

I shook my head. "They're watching television. The funeral."

"Even still. I know she's anxious to see you. Let's try to get home before dark." We started down Main Street, going past one closed shop after another.

I looked up at my father. I hated to ask, but needed to know. "Do you have a girlfriend?"

"No, darling, of course not. Your mother is the only woman for me."

Did I believe him? Not quite. I knew that adults lied, parents even. "Where have you been staying?"

"I've been sleeping in an empty cell at the station. Not too comfortably."

I couldn't let it go. He still wasn't making sense. "But why have you been so late all those nights?"

"They cut back my time at the station. The chief's nephew—they gave the boy half my hours."

"That's not fair."

"Ah sweetheart, if life were fair, JFK wouldn't be dead now, would he?" My father kissed the top of my head. "So, I took a part-time job as a janitor at the high school. Cleaning toilets."

"The perfume. I heard Ma yelling about perfume."

My father gave a sad smile. "Yes, 'perfume like disinfectant' was actually Clorox."

I suppose I should have felt relief, but instead I was furious. Why did my parents have to be so dumb? "Why didn't you just tell her?"

"She didn't intend to marry a janitor. We've been hoping I'd get on the force, maybe make detective some day. Instead, I was pushing a mop. I couldn't face her or your grandmother, either."

"But why were you so drunk?" If my father had been my child, I'm sure I would have punished him for pure stupidity.

"Felt depressed. Guess I can't hold my liquor."

"I'll say." I didn't want to be disrespectful, but it was all I could do to hold my tongue.

We paused by a shop full of televisions. Even though the store was closed, several of the sets were on, replaying scenes of the funeral. We watched for a minute. Without sound, I especially noticed the faces, all sad, all in shock, all holding questions with no answers.

Finally, my father tugged at my sleeve. We continued in silence for a while. Then he said, "It may not look like it, but your mother and I, we're trying." He paused. "I'm not perfect, Jemma."

Not perfect? Not by a long shot. My *scream first, ask later* mother wasn't perfect, either. And Nonnie, God help anybody who crossed her. "I know. Nobody's perfect."

Come to think of it, for the first time, it hit me that maybe I wasn't perfect. I was no big expert on running the universe.

I squeezed my father's hand and said, "Well, I guess you're perfect enough."

The sun started to set. As we made our way, the cold November sky bled red and then purple into the horizon.

If I'd had the power to write my life like the stories I wrote by flashlight late at night, I would have gone ahead and given myself a happy ending, right there and then. But I didn't have that power and knew I never would. Instead, on that saddest of sad days when the whole world seemed to be weeping, I held my father's hand and walked slowly toward home.

Brave Girl

Jody Hobbs Hesler

(Third place fiction, Blue Ridge Writers VWC, 2014)

Marnie wanted to know if she'd have to tell the story at the awards ceremony. "No, honey," her mother said. "Nobody expects an eight-year-old to talk to a great big crowd. The mayor will do all the talking." She zipped Marnie into the neatly pressed white dress with flowers embroidered at the chest, the one Marnie had picked out with her grandmother at Nordstrom in Richmond just for this occasion.

Over breakfast Marnie's tummy bubbled while she tried to chew and swallow her toast. "Will there be a lot of people there?"

"A good many, I suppose," her mother answered. "And TV crews and reporters, too. That's why we got you the pretty dress. That's why Grandma did your hair yesterday."

On Marnie's head, every last hair was neatly accounted for. She'd spent two hours watching *Shrek* and *Finding Nemo* the day before while her grandmother sat behind her, pulling and twisting all of her hair into tight little cornrows, with white satin ribbons hanging from every one.

"Will they talk about it?" Marnie asked. Ever since the accident, it was hard to go anywhere at all without a lot of people wanting to talk about it.

"I imagine so," her mother said. "Everyone will want to know what such a little girl did that was so brave."

"Do we have to go?"

"Of course we have to go," Marnie's mother said. "When the mayor gives you an award, least you can do is go on and get it." Her mother looked at her then the same way she did when she checked Marnie for a fever. "You're going to be just fine, sweetie, all right? This is your special day. There's nothing to be nervous about."

In the car Marnie's mother sat next to her in the backseat, holding her hand the whole way. Marnie was glad her grandmother was driving.

"The mayor said you'll be sitting up on the stage," Marnie's mother told her. "Up there with all the other folks getting the bravery award today." She went on to tell Marnie about the things the other people had done. One man had rescued a little boy from a fire and then ran back inside and rescued his yellow lab, too. A woman got a bunch of people in her neighborhood to march around one night to keep the drug dealers off their streets.

"I didn't do anything like that," Marnie said. In her lap, she rubbed her hands together. They were sweaty.

In the front seat, her grandmother chuckled. She had round cheeks and bushy gray hair. She smelled like onions and mothballs. "Girl," she said, "you the bravest of all."

Beside her in the backseat, Marnie's mother laid one hand over Marnie's hands. "Don't worry now. Nobody's going to bite you. You did something special. People like to say thank you. I like to say thank you." She squeezed Marnie's hands, and her eyes shone when Marnie looked at her.

They parked the car in the parking garage, the same way they did anytime they went downtown. But they didn't make their usual beeline for milkshakes and grilled cheeses at The Nook. They walked up some steps to glass doors that said City Space instead.

Inside, people flowed around the rooms, all grown-ups except for Marnie. Their mostly white faces loomed up over her. Marnie looked down at their shoes and at the swirly designs on the purple carpet, clutching her mother's hand and pressing herself close against her to hide herself. But that didn't stop the mayor from finding them at last. He bent down and put his pale, puffy face right into hers. His heavy hand patted her shoulder. "Here's our brave girl," he said.

Marnie's mother always told her it wasn't polite to correct people. "If someone asks you for your opinion," she said, "it's OK to give it. But don't make people feel bad, telling them they're wrong." So Marnie didn't tell the mayor, and she hadn't told any of the neighbors or reporters either, that she hadn't been brave at all, but terrified.

Marnie pressed her lips tight and stared back at the

mayor, trying not to look afraid now. His hand still on her shoulder, he nudged her toward the front of the room, down an aisle through rows and rows of chairs, toward the stage. Her mother nodded that it was OK for her to go with the mayor, and Marnie left her and her grandmother behind in the crowd.

Some people were already sitting. Others held plates of crackers and cheese and fruit while they talked. Grown-ups were forever talking to one another. Marnie had tried talking like that with her friends on the bus on the way home from school, but she could never come up with enough to say to make it all the way home.

At the front of the room, a short line of chairs faced the rows of chairs Marnie had just walked through. Three of those chairs had grown ups in them who were as dressed up as Marnie. The woman wore a flowing dress the same color as the carpet. Her skin was nearly the same tone as Marnie's, making her one of only a handful of people in the room who looked like anyone in her own family. The two men wore suits and looked like men you might see at a bank.

They must all be getting the award, too, so they must have done something brave, or at least something everyone thought was brave. Marnie knew that people didn't always know the difference. The mayor motioned for Marnie to sit in one of the empty chairs.

Marnie sat down next to one of the men who looked like a banker. He leaned toward Marnie. "So you're the brave girl I've heard all about?" People always told Marnie they'd heard all about her. At least this time she might have already heard about this man, too, which felt more even. Probably he was one of the people her mother told her about on the way here. "How did you know how to drive a car?" he asked.

This was the question everybody always asked about what happened. But of course Marnie hadn't known what she was doing. "I just did what my mommy always does," Marnie answered. It was the easiest way to explain it, and her answer had become a reflex by now.

When her mother had her seizure—Marnie had learned what to call it afterward—her eyes had bugged out like a frog's. Marnie's first reaction had been to laugh. Her mother always made silly faces at her, though not usually while she was driving. But her mother went from frog eyes to closed eyes and then fell over in the front seat, so Marnie's laughs froze up in her throat.

After that, most of what Marnie remembered was the color white—the kind of white that happens when you open your eyes onto a very snowy day, so bright you can't make out what you're looking at. There was the color white and a great screeching noise of all the sounds of the world seeming to mix up right inside her head.

Somewhere in the middle of all the white and noise, Marnie had managed to slip out of her backseat booster chair and into the front seat, onto her mother's lap. She knew only one thing—that her mother needed help. So she did whatever she had to, though she couldn't remember seeing or hearing a single thing the whole time.

Everybody always asked her what happened and how she'd known what to do. But she hadn't understood what was happening then, and she hadn't known what to do. In the end, the car had come to a stop in the middle of a clump of bushes on somebody's front lawn. A police officer had to yank open the car door and get in beside Marnie to wrench her fingers off the steering wheel. Soon after that, the emergency workers arrived. They strapped Marnie into a seat right next to her mother in the ambulance. The first clear thing Marnie remembered from that day was seeing their car tangled up in the bushes just before the emergency worker shut the ambulance doors and cut off her view.

The mayor tapped the microphone to get everyone's attention. There was a dull thud and a whirring ring before the mayor began to talk. Marnie listened to what he said about how brave the people sitting beside her had been. The man next to her had been out for his morning run when he noticed that the apartment building he was running past was on fire. Before the woman in the flowy purple had led that march in her neighborhood, stray gunfire from drug dealers having some kind of turf war had killed her son in her own front yard. These people had known exactly what they were doing, had done it on purpose.

The blur of onlookers in all the chairs in front of Marnie

kept clapping every time the mayor listed one more good thing the people sitting beside her had done, and when he got to Marnie—he saved her for last—the people clapped even louder. It was almost as loud as that day in the car.

The mayor said, "What amazing grace under pressure for an eight-year-old child," and the people nodded at her, smiling and showing so many white, white teeth. "She slipped onto her mother's lap. . . ." She'd slid onto her mother's lap, but her feet couldn't reach the pedals, and she didn't know what to do with the pedals anyway. ". . . and she kept that car on the road . . ." And there had been a truck, coming at them, straight at them, and it made a loud, loud noise before it swerved, or they swerved, and then came the bushes. ". . . until she managed to pull up in Ella and Tom Lewis' front yard." Her heart had been thudding so loud and hard it felt like a man with a hammer under her skin. "All by herself, this young lady saved her mother's life." But she hadn't, she really hadn't. Anything could have gone wrong, and it could go wrong again. And where was her mother right now? Marnie couldn't see her because of all the people and their smiley white teeth and the noise of the clapping.

The crowd swooped to its feet, clapping even more, when the mayor said, "Let's give little Marnie one more round of applause," and it felt like all the sounds of the world were crashing in on her, that she was in a car hurtling toward shapes and shadows she couldn't understand. All she could see was white again.

She wasn't brave. She was terrified, all the time. It took tiny blue pills to get her to sleep at night. She could hardly pay attention at school. One night after the accident, she'd gotten so scared she'd even wet the bed.

But the people kept clapping. They didn't know that, more than anything, she wished none of it had ever happened. She'd even once wished she hadn't been in the car that day. But if Marnie hadn't been in the car, her mother would've died. Their car would've run straight into that truck. That's what all the witnesses said. So, immediately, she'd unwished that.

The next thing Marnie remembered, the man next to her was leaning close and saying something to her. She was bent over her own lap with her eyes squinched tight, grasping her chair's front legs so hard her hands hurt. It took her a minute to hear what the man was saying to her.

He was saying "Little girl?" very softly, and, when Marnie forced her eyes open, she could see that he was bent forward at the same angle she was. "Little girl? Are you OK?"

Marnie held tight to the chair, looking toward the floor and the man's shiny black shoes and the bravery award dangling from her neck on a red, white, and blue ribbon. How had that gotten around her neck? Had she stood up and walked over to the mayor? Had the mayor come over here and hung it on her while she sat folded up in her own lap?

"Are you OK?" the man in the black suit said again.

Around them, crowds of people were still standing, talking and eating more food. Marnie couldn't answer.

"Do you know that every time I run past that building where I rescued the boy, I have to slow down and walk?" the man said. "Every time, I could swear I smell smoke."

Marnie's eyes were wide open now. She could feel the air going in and out of her again. "Really?"

The man in the black suit nodded. "That's why I keep running past there, to remind myself it's not happening anymore. One day I'll remember even before I run past."

Marnie felt a hand on her shoulder. The weight of it, and the scent that came with it, told her it was her mother's hand. The man next to her stood up and smiled at her before he walked off the stage.

A little at a time, Marnie loosened her grip on the chair legs and sat up. "I was afraid," she said, looking up at her mother.

Her mother crouched beside her. Water puddled in the corners of her eyes. "I know you were, sweetie," she said, and her voice wobbled. "But it's all over now."

The Invisibles

Gary D. Kessler

She hadn't even wanted the bracelet. She'd just never had anything that nice before, even though it wasn't her style. Not that she had a style. She deserved something and didn't think anyone would notice that she took it, because she was used to being overlooked, to just not being seen. And if no one noticed, who was there to care? There were a lot of other bracelets hanging there; one shouldn't have been missed. It would have been nice if Shayla hadn't seen her lift that bracelet, though. Shayla was supposed to be a friend of hers. Shayla took her summer job entirely too seriously, Cindy Sue thought. Not something you should go out of your way to call out a friend on. Shayla could have just looked the other way. Those stores made allowances for losing things. And how much could a bracelet from a Dollar Store be worth anyway?

It had been her birthday. The day after her birthday, actually. Neither her mother nor that good-for-nothing boyfriend of her mother's had so much as wished her a good day. Jake had made a pass at her, but there wasn't anything unusual in that—or personal, she didn't allow. Jake would spike any female who would have him or who couldn't outsmart or outrun him. Cindy Sue didn't know why her mother kept him around. It's not like he brought any money into the house. But then he was a lot younger than her mother and good looking too. Thought a lot of himself, he did. Of course, quite a few of the girls thought a lot of him too. She bet they all thought she was letting Jake mess with her. It was the only time she got any attention from them, though—them wanting to know about him and what he did with a girl. So, she just smiled a "knowing" smile when they brought it up.

Cindy Sue stopped, out of breath from the climb. She looked around. She'd been following Mine Branch up into the Blue Ridge from Crimora, but now that she looked around, she realized the stream had petered out. She wondered how long she'd been following a disappearing trickle of water. She sat down on a rock and let the backpack fall to the moss beside her.

She'd run right out of the Dollar Store, with Shayla hollering bloody murder at her back, and went straight home; threw her cell phone, some panties, a pair of shorts, and a couple of T-shirts, and enough food for a string of days in her backpack. Then she'd hauled on out of there. Her mother was at work. And, thank god, Jake wasn't anywhere around. She didn't have time to fight him off with a broom before she had to be on her way.

She guessed they'd figure she'd head south to become lost in Waynesboro, so she headed east for the mountains. That was a laugh, though. She could stand, naked in the center of Crimora and no one in town would see her.

She hadn't even come away with the bracelet. She'd let that drop on the sidewalk outside the store entrance. She'd figured anyone following her would stop to pick it up and would give her enough of a head start. Her birthday and she couldn't even give herself a present.

It had taken her three days to get this far, nearly to the top of the ridge of the Blue Ridge mountains. She was tired and her feet were screaming at her. She hadn't talked to another solitary soul in that whole time. It was just like she didn't exist.

She checked the bars in the cell phone. They were strong enough for a call. Once she was over the top of the ridge she didn't know if she could get reception. She punched in Brenda's number. Brenda was maybe her only friend, and that seemed only to hold when it suited Brenda and there were no better prospects around.

"Brenda, it's me."

"Me who?"

"Cindy Sue."

"Hi, there, Cissy. Haven't heard from you in a couple of days. Been hanging out with that boyfriend of your mother's?"

Brenda didn't sound surprised or excited or anything. "I'm on a trip. Anybody been asking for me?"

"Not that I've heard. Did you hear about Rachel? She's carrying, and she says it's Pete Winter's. Can you imagine that?"

73

"No, do tell. The bus looks like it's ready to pull out, so I gotta go. Just was checking in."

"Bus?"

Cindy Sue didn't respond. She'd already clicked off. Nobody had missed her. Maybe after Shayla had calmed down, she hadn't said anything to anybody about the bracelet after all.

She was still on this side of the ridge. She could just turn around and go home. To what, though?

She looked around. It was peaceful up here. And so green and quiet. Really beautiful. She decided she'd rest right here and climb that last little bit tomorrow.

By noon of the next day, she was at the summit. She knew that because she was standing next to the Skyline Drive and the terrain dipped down the mountainside both east and west of that. She retreated back below a rock wall when she heard a car coming down the drive, and then, when it had passed, she dashed across the road and started downhill. Charlottesville. She'd go down into Charlottesville, get a job, and be someone people noticed. Maybe she'd dye her hair pink and get a nose ring.

The middle of the next day she sensed she knew where she was. Before he'd disappeared, her dad had brought the kids to the Sugar Hollow Reservoir a couple of times and then on upstream from there to a multichambered swimming hole carved out of the rocks. Her dad had been fun—when he was around. He'd noticed her. He looked directly at her, not through her, and he'd actually ask her questions. He just didn't stay around for the answers.

She floated in the water of the swimming hole. She hadn't bathed for what, nearly a week now? How long had she been gone? Was it five days now or six?

And no one had come looking for her.

It was nice, real nice here at the swimming hole. She could just live here forever. Get herself a nice little cabin and just live away from the world in these beautiful mountains. Go off the grid, not that it seemed she ever was on it. Bet nobody would find her.

She heard voices coming up the trail and scampered out of the water, grabbed her clothes, and melted into the trees.

The voices were a jolt. Other than the phone call with Brenda, she hadn't talked to or seen anyone for nearly a week now.

She wanted to talk with someone—to connect—but not with any strings or fuss. She wasn't far from the summit, so after pulling her clothes on, she climbed back up there. When she got there, she could have kicked herself for not checking her bars before making the effort. But the cell phone was still good. She called Brenda again.

"You didn't tell me you'd run off, Cissy," Brenda said. Her voice was breathless and sounded excited now, as if she was at the center of something. "Where are you? There are posters out on you. The cops have asked me about you twice. Came to school and then to my house. All the guys at school are asking me about you. Your mother's boyfriend has been pulled in and they're talking to him about where you might be."

Just like Brenda, Cindy Sue thought. Always making it all about her. "So, my mother is looking for me?"

"Not that I've heard. It was your grandmother. You were supposed to up and babysit for her in Grottoes or something. They're saying your mother didn't even know you were missing. Or so she claimed."

"Have you told anybody you talked with me? Did you tell the cops that?"

"No. I didn't know if you'd want me to. But, like I said, they're questioning your mother's boyfriend."

"Good. Don't tell anybody we've talked yet, OK? I don't know if I want to come back." She clicked off before Brenda could ask any more questions.

She knew she shouldn't have left the conversation like that. But if her mother hadn't even known she was gone . . . and if her grandmother's main concern was being out of a babysitter. . . . Maybe she'd just let them stew a bit. Be invisible for a while. And most of the heat seemed to be on Jake. Good, he deserved it.

She started back down the eastern slope of the Blue Ridge. A couple of more days and she was down, past the reservoir, and on flat ground again. She also was out of food and was hungry. If she'd had decent hiking boots on she could have

75

moved faster. But she hadn't even thought about what was on her feet when she scrammed out of there.

She walked to an intersection that claimed it was the town of White Hall, but there wasn't much more than a general store and a few houses and a narrow road dumping into a wider road. The narrow road didn't even cross the wider one; it just dumped into an old general store. A general store was what she wanted, though. It wasn't a bracelet she needed to lift anymore. Now it was food and maybe a six-pack of Coke. She was hungry—and not just for attention or thinking she deserved a birthday present, even if she had to steal it herself because no one else remembered it was her birthday.

She entered the store and started walking the aisles. There was a young guy—pretty good looking, but shy like—at the cash register. He was watching her every move, so she guessed this wasn't going to be an easy proposition.

The word "Crimora" hit her face from a copy of the Waynesboro newspaper that was on a stand just inside the store entrance. She went over and looked at it. The face of Brenda stared back at her. It had been an auto accident. Drinking had been involved. Brenda hadn't been driving, but she was the one who was dead. The only person Cindy Sue had talked to since she herself had disappeared, and now she was dead. Cindy Sue wondered if Brenda really had had the time or inclination to say anything before the accident about her having called. But she thought not. Brenda had always liked to have secrets—at least until she got people's full attention. Sure, she would have blabbed, but only after a couple of days of "I've got a secret" tease. Cindy Sue thought she should work up some tears for Brenda's passing, but she was just too weary and hungry at this moment. Maybe later. Brenda would just have to wait. She always made Cindy Sue wait to see if they were still friends on any given week.

* * * *

Zeb woke up to the silence. He listened for his mother's steady breathing from the other room, but then he remembered. He'd buried his mother three weeks earlier. Nobody else even to stand with him while he looked for the right words in the family Bible. He was all alone now in Bobcat Hollow. Not another soul in here now. There never had been more than his family. This was the way his people wanted it, but Zeb didn't think that any of them had ever thought the family would get down to just one. And even if so, they'd likely not to have been pleased to learn it was him. He wasn't the one the rest of the family had seen much of any promise in.

He lived in a two-over-two house that had been here since before the war of northern aggression. It was stuck deep in the hollow, where nothing but a trail that you had to know was there to see it led. Zeb had to walk three miles just to get to where he stashed his old Ford 150 pickup. You could be flying right over the house and not know it was there.

That's what Zeb's folks, the Walkers, had counted on for nearly ninety years now. It was back in the 1920s when some folks up in Washington decided that the Blue Ridge down to Rockfish Gap needed to be a national park. They didn't ask any of the folks who had settled and lived in those mountains for nearly three centuries what they thought of that idea, though. Ten years after deciding that, they decided that the mountain folk all had to go. For the next decade, they bought folks out, and those who wouldn't go were pushed and pulled out, so that by 1940 they declared that there were fewer than a hundred folks still living in the mountains and that they were so hard to catch up with that they could just die out in place.

What the people in Washington didn't know, though, was that it was going to take a lot longer than that for the people of the hollows to give up their way of life.

Zeb's folks, down from his grandparents, had just ignored the outside world and stuck back up in Bobcat Hollow in a fold between Pinestand and Cedar mountains. Zeb's granddaddy had made do with a plot of farmland they owned and worked in the valley west of Pasture Fence Mountain. And his daddy had ventured down into the White Hall area to help with the harvests. The Walker women, though, back as far as anyone had talked about, had stayed right here in the hollow, from the day they were born to the day they died.

Three families had been sticking out the evictions in that hollow, and doing so because the government agents didn't even know where this hollow was. They had married and bickered among themselves. And then only one family remained, taking great pride that it was the last. And now Zeb was all alone.

He'd worked a couple of years down in White Hall, at the general store there, and would continue to do so. But his heart was right here in Bobcat Hollow.

It was sort of lonely, though, without even his mother to come home to. And now there was so much to do to keep the homestead going. He did miss his mother. He wasn't fond of a lot of yakking, but it was nice to have someone to talk to in the evenings. His mother had been good that way; she never was a yakker. She had been dead in her rocking chair the better part of a day before Zeb realized she'd passed.

Working in the White Hall general store wasn't too bad. Not too many folks came in, and most of those who did looked right through him—like he was invisible. They did their business and were gone.

He'd heard that some years before he'd come to work here there had been a group of old men who sat out on the store's front porch and jawed and chawed and rocked the day away. But they were all gone. And none of the younger men had replaced them. They all were going east, into Charlottesville, or south, to Crozet, to work—even if they came back to White Hall to live. But not many were staying here now even to sleep the night.

And no one asked him where he lived. No one asked him much of anything other than the price of something that had been missed in the labeling.

He liked it that way. Still he missed his mother. And someone to share the chores with up in Bobcat Hollow.

He hadn't allowed time for firing up the cook stove. It would take him time to remember that he had to get up earlier if he wanted a hot breakfast on weekdays. He grabbed a couple of chunks of bread from the breadbox, pulled the jug of milk up from the cool stream running through the basement of the house, and poured himself a glass. And then he was off, down slope on the narrow trail to where he kept the pickup.

When he got to the store, he opened up and brought in the papers—the *Daily Progress* from Charlottesville and the *Waynesboro News Virginian* from the other side of the mountains. He brought them inside and placed them on the stand inside the door. He clucked his tongue at the sad news on the front of the Waynesboro paper about the young girl killed in the automobile accident over in Crimora. Liquor. That's why his parents and their parents had stuck to the hills, his mother always told him. Because young people were too anxious about killing themselves over something they had no business being into.

He noticed that a flyer had dropped out of one of the Waynesboro papers and he stooped down and picked it up.

More troubled girls. A nice looking girl, another one from Crimora, missing. He'd read about that in the Waynesboro paper the previous day. Obviously the mother's boyfriend was suspected. She was a good-looking girl in the photo on the flyer, but she looked sad. If he was going to put another word to it, he'd say she looked lonely. He felt sorry for her. Lost and probably never would be found. Invisible, just like him. The report said she'd gone missing right after her birthday. That made it all the sadder.

He went behind the counter and moved a vase of flowers more to the right, away from where folks would put their purchases down on the counter when he rang them up. That Mrs. Stevens, who worked the evenings. She had to have something to cheer the place up. She'd bring in flowers every day. These were yellow roses—probably from her own garden. They'd still be there in the morning, and Zeb always had to move them to the side.

As he was doing this, he heard the door open and a young woman walked in. He recognized her immediately. He'd just seen her in the missing person's brochure, and the face, which had haunted him a bit with the aspect of the same loneliness he was feeling, had stuck with him. Cindy Sue something was her name. She'd just had a birthday.

He watched her move around the store. And he watched her giving him furtive glances. He wondered if she found him attractive. He thought he could find her attractive. If she'd just give some hint of a smile. She looked scared, though, and hungry. Her sneakers were in a tatters, and she was walking gingerly. It dawned on him that she wasn't there to shop, really—that she, in fact, was hungry and didn't have the money to buy anything. He couldn't remember how long she'd been missing, but he thought maybe it had been a week or more. Had she had anything to eat in that time? How had she gotten over the mountain? Had she hitchhiked? White Hall wasn't really on any driven route over the mountains. Had she maybe walked over the mountain? All alone the whole time? In those sneakers?

She went over to the newspaper stand, and he could see she was looking at the story on the girl who died in the auto wreck. Another girl from Crimora. He wondered if this Cindy Sue had known the other girl. Crimora wasn't much more of a town than White Hall was. They probably had known each other. He couldn't tell if she was working toward tearing up or something.

He had the sudden wish that she would open the paper and see the missing person poster—to see that someone missed her. That she wasn't invisible like Zeb thought about himself. But then, with a glimmer of thought and wondering if Cindy Sue would like the house in Bobcat Hollow, he hoped she wouldn't open the paper.

To keep her from doing that, he cleared this throat, pulled a rose out of the vase, and spoke up. "Miss, you look like you could use a yellow rose. I think this would look pretty in your hair."

Cindy Sue looked up, surprised. But she also was pleased, and she gave Zeb a tentative smile.

"You look like you might be hungry too. Why don't you just pick out something you'd like to eat. And we have soft drinks in the cooler over there. We'll pretend it's your birthday or something."

"It . . . it *was* my birthday just the other day, as a matter of fact," Cindy Sue answered. And her smile broadened.

The Magic Sweatshirt

Brenda A. Morris

The year I was fourteen Edward and I didn't get anything for Christmas. We didn't even have a meal that was different from the cornbread and beans that was our usual meal. If Daddy had money to celebrate Christmas, he didn't share any of it with us. He didn't even share the day with us.

Someone in the community must have known how dire our circumstances were, for the ladies of the church came the day after Christmas with a box of clothes they'd collected for us. They weren't new, but they were more than we had before. In that box were some patched pants for Edward and a couple shirts. For me there were some worn dresses and a sweatshirt. A shining, white sweatshirt. I'd never seen anything so pure white, for anything white I owned took on the beige color of the water from the creek from which I had to carry my wash water. Yet here was this used sweatshirt, still as snow white as it was when it was new. I was afraid to wear it because if I had to wash it, I'd never get it back to the purity it held now.

When school resumed after the break, everyone seemed to be wearing something new. Of course, I wore the same threadbare dress I'd worn before the break. Betty Jean, who'd always been sort of nice to me before, caught me in the hall.

"Christine, what did you get for Christmas?" she asked. Her question seemed innocent enough, except I noticed she wasn't asking any of the other girls that question. Then I noticed the hall had fallen silent after she asked. I didn't want to look around me, to see the questioning, and I was afraid, mocking eyes that were watching me.

I'm sure my mama, if she'd still been alive, would have said the Devil got a hold of me at that moment. But Mama had been gone for over six years. So I became Cinderella and that white sweatshirt was my great coach with four bay horses, a footman, and a driver.

"I got a white cashmere sweater," I said. "It's so soft. Of course, it's too expensive to wear to school. I can only wear it for special occasions."

Betty Jean was stunned. She hadn't expected an answer like that from me, and the response she had planned to say sat like rocks in her mouth.

I smiled at everyone and walked down the hall in my well-worn, old dress as if I were a queen.

In my heart I knew what I had done was wrong, and Mama would have chastised me for creating such a lie. Silently I prayed to her," Mama, forgive me. I try to be good but sometimes it's just too hard." I carried my beautiful white, cashmere sweater with me throughout that day, a shield against the arrows of words that people wanted to use to hurt me.

Blue Christmas

Olivia Stowe

"Well, all right, I guess I could do that." Clara tried to make her reluctance quite clear, but Elizabeth was having none of that. She just cheerily plowed along, working on getting Clara on the road to fill in for no-shows among the volunteers at the soup kitchen where Elizabeth was working that evening.

Nothing had put her off—not Clara's remark that it was already dark, not her observation that it had begun to snow—not even the noting that it was Christmas Eve.

Everyone knew Clara didn't come out on Christmas Eve—that she hadn't done so for nearly a decade. Everyone but Elizabeth, apparently. But that wasn't Elizabeth's fault. She'd only moved here last summer, and no one talked about Clara and Christmas Eve any more. And Elizabeth was such a gem. She'd been there for Clara on short notice so many times herself. Clara knew she owed Elizabeth big time, and Elizabeth wasn't being pushy so much as she was assuming that her good friend would do what Elizabeth would do for anyone else in a short-notice bind like this.

Clara couldn't say no—and in the end she didn't. She promised she'd be there. Elizabeth just didn't understand about Clara and Christmas Eve. Clara knew Elizabeth would be the first one to understand and to be sensitive if she knew.

It started as soon as Clara entered the garage. For some time after that she wondered why she hadn't just stopped trying at that point. As the door into the house shut and locked, Clara realized she didn't have her car keys—or her house keys for that matter. She had an emergency house key hidden in the garage, of course, although it took her a couple of minutes to remember where she'd put it. But she did remember—and in the precious moments she lost in reentering the house and retrieving her car keys and getting the garage door lifted, the snow had begun to stick on the driveway.

"Remember that Elizabeth sounded almost desperate for the help and that she has put everything down to help me so often," Clara muttered to herself as she pulled out of the garage. It would have been hard enough on any snowy night. But it was Christmas Eve. Everyone knew Clara hid away on Christmas Eve. Everyone but Elizabeth. But Elizabeth needed her. She'd said that fewer volunteers had shown up at the soup kitchen than anticipated, but more of the homeless than planned had come in off the street to escape the cold and the snow—and to have some semblance of family on Christmas Eve.

Family on Christmas Eve, Clara thought. And, whether she wanted them to or not, the tears started to roll down her cheeks as she drove out into the dark night.

Clara rolled up to St. Mark's Presbyterian Church on Maple—almost on the other side of town—to find very few cars in the parking lot. This was a surprise, as Elizabeth had said the church was running Christmas programs all evening and their meal and shelter service for the homeless was being hampered by everyone bringing in cookies for the breaks between the church services and competing for counter space in the kitchen.

Clara stepped out of the car—and into a slushy puddle, realizing only then that she hadn't put on her snow boots before she'd left home. And when she got to the door of the church, she found only a group of people finishing putting up the decorations for the late-evening church services.

Clara was almost choked up with the emotion of being in a church for the first time on Christmas Eve in eight years, and it took her several minutes—after having gone into the community building wing and finding the kitchen dark—to build up the capability to return to the sanctuary and query one of those there what the problem was.

"Oh, you must mean St. Mark's Lutheran across town on Landon Street," a cheery, rosy-cheeked woman answered. "I think they are on for the homeless shelter duty over the holidays. We'd be pleased if you attended one of our services here, of course. It's only a little more than an hour before the first of those."

"Uh . . . no thanks," Clara stammered. "Thanks, but no thanks. I don't go to Christmas Eve services anymore. I . . . I can't . . ." By then Clara had backed up to the outer door in the narthex, though, and she turned and fled into the cold, snowy night.

It had been her own fault. She had just latched onto the St. Mark's name when Elizabeth had mentioned where help was needed. Elizabeth probably even had specified it was St. Mark's Lutheran and Clara had been so focused on forming her excuses for not coming that she hadn't paid attention. No wonder Elizabeth thought it wouldn't be much of an imposition, Clara thought. St. Mark's Lutheran was near where Clara had started out from home. Elizabeth had every reason to assume that the snow wouldn't be that much of a problem for Clara.

Clara looked up at the sky. The snowflakes were getting larger and there was increasingly less space between them as they fell. She decided it would be best to take the country road around the perimeter of the town rather than drive through town with all of the rest of the sliding cars.

Bad decision.

Half way around town, on a pitch-black stretch of road going through a thickly forested section, a deer bounded across the road just beyond Clara's headlights and she pulled hard to the right to avoid it. She missed the deer, but she glanced off a boulder at the side of the road with her wheel, and she didn't get more than a couple of hundred yards farther down the road before her tire blew and the car lurched into a side ditch.

"I knew it," Clara moaned. "I knew I shouldn't have tried to come out on Christmas Eve." All of the hurt and frustration and despair of this one night of the year boiled up inside her and Clara was crying again. Big, gasping, gobs of crying—almost wailing. But almost as soon as it had started, it stopped. Clara had controlled herself for eight years; she wasn't going to fall to pieces on Christmas Eve now. She'd call AAA and just get them to take her home. She had borne up under the burden for eight years. She would continue to tough it out.

She was dialing the cell phone under the weak light of the ceiling dome when she heard the tapping on her window.

"Can I help?" a man asked through the pane of glass.

He looked familiar. Yes, she'd seen him in the group of folks she'd gone to the theater with as Elizabeth's guest the week after Thanksgiving. He'd been sweet. A great smile and funny

85

stories. It had been a group from Elizabeth's church, Clara remembered. She rolled down the window.

"Say, aren't you Mrs. Benton?" he asked.

"Yes, yes," Clara answered. "And you're Ben . . . Ben from Elizabeth Sturges' church group, aren't you?"

"Yes. It looks like you are in a good bit of trouble and that you won't be going anywhere in this car tonight."

"I was just calling AAA," Clara answered.

"Maybe you should do that," Ben answered. "I'd change your tire for you, but it looks like you have some front end damage too."

"I hit a rock—avoiding a deer," Clara said.

"Ah. Well, you can get AAA out here and then I'll drive you anywhere you want to go."

"I don't live that far away," Clara answered. "But where were you headed? I don't want you to be late . . . on Christmas Eve."

"I'm going to church; to St. Mark's on Landon. Helping with some of the church services there this evening."

"Ah," Clara said. She dreaded the thought, but she couldn't forget the help she'd promised to Elizabeth, and her White Knight was headed there already. It seemed to be fate. Clara gave in to it.

"That's where I was originally headed too, actually," Clara admitted. "Elizabeth enlisted me to help with the meal service for the homeless tonight. So, if you want, we could just go there and you could take me home afterward . . . if that wouldn't be an imposition." She almost wished that he'd say it was and she could opt for him taking her home instead.

"That would be great," Ben said. "You'd even have time to go to a service after the kitchen closed down . . . if you liked."

Clara began to tremble, and she barely was able to control her voice when she answered. "I don't really go to Christmas Eve services anymore. If there was someplace I could just wait until you were ready to leave—"

"Sure, sure, no problem," Ben quickly said. And his smile was genuine, so Clara didn't feel she had to make any further excuses.

When they arrived at the church, Elizabeth expressed delight at seeing Clara and clucked sympathetically at the story of how difficult it had been for Clara to get there, but she didn't really seem to be all that much in need of help.

"Some volunteers came in who weren't scheduled," she said. "Just wanted to help out on Christmas Eve. But if you could, Clara, I'd appreciate it if you'd take a meal over to that young man sitting at the table by himself. He didn't come through the food line; just got some coffee, and we'll be closing the line down soon. He looks pretty dejected; I'm sure he needs the meal and a friendly face."

Clara took a tray of food and approached the young man in dread. There was a familiarity about him—even in the way his head was hanging, and his shoulders looked just about ready to collapse into his chest.

"Oh, dear god, not on Christmas Eve," Clara murmured as she approached. On top of everything else she just didn't think she could manage this on Christmas Eve. But she supposed she'd have to.

"Hi," she said.

"Hi to you too," the young man said. When he looked up, there was a familiar sadness in his eyes, and Clara immediately knew that she wouldn't leave him alone. Not on Christmas Eve. She somehow knew this was another chance being given her.

"I brought you some food," she said. And when she set it down on the table at his elbow, she sat down across from him herself. "The kitchen is about to close, and they say you haven't eaten yet."

"Don't need it, thanks. But thanks for bringing it. I'll take the coffee; mine is about all gone."

"Well, maybe you'll feel like eating in a bit," Clara said. "Do you mind if I sit? I've had quite an evening, and it would be good to get off my feet."

"No, it's fine. I don't mind."

Little by little Clara drew the young man out in conversation, and it was no surprise to find that she was right—that the familiar look about him probably meant just what she thought it meant.

When they'd become comfortable with each other and Clara hadn't pressed too much on his evasions—getting only a sketchy "feeling inferior and abandoned by the world" version of why he was here on Christmas Eve rather than anywhere else—she reached down into her pocketbook and took a shiny silver coin out and held it up for the young man to see.

"Would you accept a small Christmas present from me?" she asked softly. "It's not worth much, I'm sure, but I've had it for several years, and I think you might appreciate it. It was my son's."

"Your son's?" the young man asked. He took the coin from her and held it up to the light. "Where's this from?" he asked. "I can't read any of the inscription. It looks fancy, though. What country is it from? And doesn't your son want it anymore?"

"That's the point of it, I think," Clara answered in a low voice that she was using every power she had to keep under control. "Erick's grandfather gave it to him, telling him that it was his job to figure out where it came from—that as long as he had such a quest facing him, he would have a purpose in life."

"Sounds deep," the young man answered. "And why do you have it?"

And then, in faltering but purposeful tones, Clara told the young man, who seemed so similar in his demeanor to her own son, of the Christmas Eve eight years previously when she and her husband had bustled off to church services—not even bothering to listen to why her son, who had been despondent for so long, wasn't going to go with them. And then, how they had come home after midnight to find that he had hanged himself in his room—that he had died, despondent, and all alone on Christmas Eve—while they were at a church service.

"I should have known," Clara said as she at last struggled through the telling of that story. "I was just too busy with getting everything just right for Christmas. But I should have known. I found this coin in the trash can in my bedroom three days before Christmas. I should have known that Erick was trying to reach out to me, was trying to tell me that he had reached the end of whatever hell he was living in. I can only imagine what that was—what it was that would go through the mind of a young man who had everything available to him in life if he just reached out for it. But I'm sure he discarded that coin where he was sure that I'd see it, where I would know that he no longer was seeking. But I was blind. And just too busy getting ready for the season. I . . . I failed him."

Clara looked up at the young man then, into his face. While she'd been telling her story, she hadn't been able to look at him. But now she wanted to know whether he had understood any of this—whether he knew why she had told him a story she'd kept locked inside her for eight years.

And the look he gave her told her that he knew why and that it had to do with him as much as her lost son—but that he was wavering on the fence.

"And your husband?" he whispered.

"He couldn't endure it. We had been living together—but apart—for some time already. He left within a year. And every Christmas since then has been what we call a Blue Christmas for me—the lowest day of the year. And I've never again decorated for Christmas or left my darkened house on Christmas Eve. At least until tonight."

The silence between them was deafening.

But Clara built up the strength to go on. Somehow she knew she had struggled in this evening for a purpose, a purpose that was beyond her control, and that she couldn't leave it this way. She was desperate to move him off that fence. It was as if this was the last chance for her—more so than for the young man.

"I've given you a present now. . . . You'll accept it, won't you? It would mean so much to me."

The young man nodded his head ever so slightly, almost indecisively, but he didn't return the coin.

"So, could I ask for a present from you?" Clara rushed on.

"I don't really have—"

"I have a cell phone here," Clara interrupted. "All I'd like for a present is that you take it and call your parents and tell them you are OK on Christmas Eve. Could you do that for me? You said they didn't live very far from here. Please? I'll move away and give you some privacy."

The young man didn't say no, and Clara put her cell phone on the table in front of him and got up and moved over to Elizabeth before he could turn her request down.

"You certainly seemed to be in serious conversation with that young man," Elizabeth said. From her tone, Clara could tell that Elizabeth was pleased—and maybe relieved. She wouldn't have been surprised to hear that Elizabeth had sought the extra help this evening precisely because of the young man and how sad and desperate he looked.

Clara turned to see that the young man was speaking into the telephone. When she turned back, Elizabeth had retreated into the church's kitchen, where they were beginning to clean up the cooking utensils and making room for an increasing stream of plates of cookies for the festivities between church services upstairs.

Clara followed her into the kitchen, and after several minutes of helping Elizabeth, she went back out into the fellowship hall. The young man had finished his call and was standing up.

He handed Clara's cell phone back to her, and she sighed when she saw that the familiar look she'd seen in his face earlier had drained away from him.

"Thanks," he said. "Thank you so much. Could you tell them over at the intake table that I won't be here for the night?"

"You're not going back out into the snow, I hope," Clara said in a concerned voice.

"No. No. My parents are coming by to pick me up in a few minutes. I'll try going home again, I guess."

Tears sprang to Clara's eyes, and she couldn't help beaming up into his face.

"Oh, and . . . um, it's awkward. But could you take this for me? I'm sorry, I don't know what else to do with it. But I don't want it anymore. Don't need it anymore, I think."

As he was saying this, he took a newspaper-wrapped parcel out of his jacket pocket. It made a clunking noise as he put it down on the table.

"And . . . and thanks for the coin. Do you want me to let you know where it came from when I've figured it out?"

"No. No, thanks," Clara answered. "I do believe I'd like to keep it in the seeking mode. Perhaps you can pass it on to someone who needs it."

Clara and Elizabeth were slipping through the narthex of the church after leaving the young man's parcel in the pastor's office with a note attached, nervous and not knowing what else to do with the hand gun the young man had left behind, when Ben came through the door to the sanctuary, which was already nearly filled with people attending the next-to-last evening service. Strains of "It Came Upon a Midnight Clear" were filtering through the church as an introit into the service.

"Oh, there you are, Clara," Ben said. "Come, I'll show you where you can wait and rest until the service is over. I'll be able to take you home after this service."

"Thank you," Clara said, "But if you don't mind, I think maybe I'll come into the service with you. I haven't been out of the house on Christmas Eve, let alone to a Christmas service, in eight years."

As soon as she uttered those words, Clara was sorry that she'd said them in Elizabeth's hearing. Now Elizabeth might learn why and feel bad that she'd brought Clara out on Christmas Eve.

But Elizabeth was at Clara's elbow and was giving a little tentative half smile. "I know you didn't, Clara. I'd heard about that. But I thought it was time that you did come out on this, of all, nights. I hope I—"

Elizabeth didn't have to finish her sentence, though, because Clara smiled and wrapped her arm under Elizabeth's and guided her into the sanctuary behind Ben, looking for three empty spaces in the overflowing pews.

POETRY

Before Your Surgery

Sharon Leiter

(Early December 2010)

I'm waiting for you
to come home and
make love to me
for the last time.

I haven't showered
or dressed. I haven't
put on makeup. I've
been sitting all day
at the computer
in my nightgown,
grading final papers.

When you come
home we will lie
down on our bed
and hold each other.

We won't require
some fancy dance
to get us there.

We are natives
of these woods.
We walk blind
to the warm cabin.

I believe the flame
we have bathed in
for fifty years
will seize us again—

unless we are simply

too sad
to tap on the door

and breathe in
the time-scented walls
as if it were yesterday

I am running away from your body

Sharon Leiter

(August 20, 2011)

I am running away from your body
not the impossible rot
in the plain pine casket
deeply carved
with a star of David

but the *you*—*David sheli*—
my Hebrew David—
sweet perfection of limbs
scent of desire—
mine since that first
separation—
when I sailed half a world away
that I might earn my right
of return to you

I am running away from your face—
the last one I loved
as much as the first
and cannot look back at
as you smile—broad cheeked
green eyed—

from the photos we always had
to be taking—I never knew why—
and know even less now

when the evidence of you
destroys me every time

A Visit

Sharon Leiter

(November 8, 2011)

I went to the Hebrew Cemetery
for the Rosh Hashanah memorial
service, stood at the place where
you lie, next to my parents'
shared gravestone. You were no more
than a slight rise in the ground,
imperceptible, had I not been looking
for you and the children placing
small stones on the spot and on
my parents' polished marking.

You were no more palpable
to me there than you are in
my spiteful dreams, though
the children, who had not
seen you lowered,
were solemn
and excited to have
some part of you at last.

At year's end,
I will raise a
stone to you,
dark,
polished,
impenetrable,
with some words
that must suffice
out of all the words.
This will disguise
the barbarity beneath
the ground,
and give me a way
to come to you.

Garden Gems

Elizabeth Doyle Solomon

Elusive jewels of flight
hovering ruby-throat bright
covering distances far,
clever avians you are!

Just seconds I see one sip,
extend a straw from its lip;
scarlet beebalm barely nods,
so gently this prober prods.

Thrust thru a summer morning
born for garden's adorning—
their forests disappearing,
close to extinction nearing.

How naked, petals and blooms
where no small hummingbird zooms;
lush habitats turned to ash
for merest handsful of cash!

Sunday in Shenandoah

Elizabeth Doyle Solomon

A black ribbon of road
climbed the rock-ridged mountains
where August wildflowers
stood tall to see us pass.

Crowds of yellow petals
surrounded pale gray cones;
bumblebees and monarchs
fed on milkweed's pale pinks.

At their feet bloomed clover:
white, purple, and least hop;
digging in a sawdust mound,
a black bear cub found insects.

Deer at the meadow's edge
had no fear as we neared;
racing the night, a red fox
streaked past in our headlights.

At the last overlook,
we observed twinkling sparks
across valley's wide floor,
a fairy land at dark.

We kissed once, then again,
our love like an amen
in this temple we call
Shenandoah Park.

Night Rain

Elizabeth Doyle Solomon

Night drops
    as if a black bowl
has been turned
    over the day

Rain falls
    silver hooves dancing
playing on
    an ebony drum.

Summer's heat
    washes with cool
and the damp
    after-midnight air
is a woman
    her long wet hair
draped upon
    the earth's bare back.

Howling Totem

Sigrid Mirabella

Listen
a dog howls
like a wolf in whelp
past the small mountain
unsettling hushed peace
nonbelievers envision is life
so fooled by their own hopes

Listen
a dog howls
like a baby entering
the world in mid morning
before an expectant rust blushes
the eastern horizon above tree lines
blessed in the birth of their own silhouettes

Listen
a dog howls
like you wish was you
far away on a mountain
where being mastered is impossible
below the free sun and rain like love
that immerses everything as if in baptism

Heart of a Wolf

Sigrid Mirabella

In the forest of just beyond,
I drop on all fours, pull on a wolf robe,
watch full moon slide above pine peaks and
clouds.

Night heightens movements, bird sighs.
Verdant growth clicks, shushes, and tremors,
snakes out from fire-cored earth,
the eloquent quiet of quarts beneath roots.
I lick my teeth growing long, saliva like water
wells over curled tongue, droplets spill to the
river.

My dark reflection under its surface ripples past.
I run to catch-up with shape-shifting self.
The moon, soon swift in full stream, unfastens
its shine to squinted wolf eyes, converts
dual-chambered beats to singular growl.

Head to sky, I howl what I know,
bite through live ribs to eat my own heart
content in my animal blood,
forever just beyond the forest I knew.

Outfoxed by the Moon

Sigrid Mirabella

No longer fully the mortal black fox,
my heart grows smaller,
faster in feline beats, faster breaths
dumbfounds transforming lungs.

And now fear arching, black fur puffing
the unstoppable change as feet pulse
into retractable claws already legendary
for their blood.

Moon colored irises float in darkness,
elliptical pupils consume stars,
question mark nostrils flare at electrified wind,
fast feet pad clay ground, run from themselves,
away from those vulpine paw prints,
singularly tracked, predator to predator.
The moon also pursues.

I throw back my head,
meowl final transmutation,
slink into horizon.

Famine Cottages: Ireland 2009

Jody Hobbs Hesler

(First place poetry, Blue Ridge Writers VWC, 2013)

It was someone's house
once—stone husk, thatchless
crumbling lump of
history.

A cow outside, and sheep;
a crop, a baby,
two, three, four—
a mother calling
all the names.

I can hear it. Sounding
down to the seas, ebbing
with the waves, puffing
through the sky: clouds,
dreams—yesterday.

All those black
potatoes, black as earth
that birthed them.
Now the peat runs
with ruts where spades dug
and plundered such fecund,
hallowed ground.

How anyone could die
here—among the wonder
of the color green—
the way it paints
the landscape lush:
the color of hope, of growth.

It was someone's house
once, someone's town,
someone's family tree
bowing now, forgotten
to the ax—All skeletons.
The houses like grave stones
crumbling in rows.

Shadows in the Sand

Linda Levokove

(Second place poetry, Blue Ridge Writers VWC, 2014)

Moonlight casts its golden glow,
egrets wheel, winged blossoms
bloom above the silent sea . . .

you reach for my hand

Palms wave leisurely, stretching
their slender seductive shadows
across the star-spattered bay . . .

you kiss impatient lips

Wildflowers shimmy in sea-grass,
bejeweled wavelets rush and brush
against our tender winter toes . . .

we sink into soft sand

Now, as the midnight bells chime
I walk the beach alone, can see
us still, as we were way back then . . .

our hands entwined

The birds have fled, the water rough,
all the tall leafy palms scarcely stir—
but the solemn shadows still linger . . .

I can taste your kiss

Withered flowers unravel in the wind,
and the tide is too cold for my toes

that are no longer quite as tender . . .

but still sink into the sand

My Child in the Moonlight

Linda Levokove

(From *Cabbages & Kings*)

Daylight swoops

down the morning sky

casts a golden flush

on porcelain cheeks

where an errant curl

of dark hair lies

and eyelids flutter

perhaps in a dream

rosebud lips smile

the tiniest bit . . .

and I fear

it is dangerous

to be so beautiful . . .

that you could silence

a skylark.

Of Flesh and Roses

Linda Levokove

(from *Cabbages & Kings*)

Every June the wild roses bloom,
tiny tight buds burst into color

surrender to the sun's warm breath
the parched petals unfold

soft puffs of dewy perfume
floating on the unsullied air

Roses, old as the soil they grow in
before their names became exotic,

pungent as the scent of desire,
long before you became a memory.

Of flesh and roses, roses and flesh . . .

when sunlight shone through slatted shutters,
your tongue lapping at my impatient flesh—

the leaves brushing against the window,
my body rising to your quicksilver touch.

Warring With Words

Lauvonda Lynn Young

(Third place poetry, Blue Ridge Writers VWC, 2014)

I oft am at war with Words
they cloak sounds in night
spread ill will at dawn
bore into brain mass
suck on artistic thought

Words cripple fingers
hold them hostage
razor sunshine from
my gnarled mind's eye

Words bombard me with
stones when I need bread
hemorrhage my bones
with repeated harangue

Wounded past of mine
is disgorged daily
cause Words don't know
the meaning of love

These Generals uncivil
dance amid doggerel
while they labor
to silence my pen

ENOUGH

I must corral these Words
entomb them in concrete
discover more, I can adore
astound myself afterward
by writing verse *de novo*

Planting Seeds

Leonard Tuchyner

(From *A Journey to Elsewhere*)

There are some who plant the seeds
to watch the green things grow,
to be affirmed in every year
that life, eternally, renews.

There are some who plant the seeds
to eat of Earth's sweet flesh,
to know that they are blessed,
within God's sacred breast.

There are some who plant the seeds
to see the crowns of nature's blooms
sing a song with bumblebees
and drink of holy hues.

But here is one who plants the seeds
to get down on his hands and knees,
touch and smell the loamy soil
and feel and play in muddy toil.

Morning Dove

Leonard Tuchyner

I sat today in my study
surrounded by shelves of books
and pondered words that I might write
reflecting on a weighty thought
and carrying a glimmer of wisdom

Suddenly the song of a mourning dove
till now not heard
in this late spring season.
One note and nothing more
pierced through bookish walls
and wakened my dusty brain

Soft though it was
it called to me sharp and clear
"You are lost still in winter's longing
day is warm and breezy
your garden is calling
come to me. I am warm and moist
sink your lover's spade into my fertile soil"

Putting down my pen
closing book covers on dry yellow paper
I took up my spade and plow

PROSE NONFICTION

Close Encounters of the Furry Kind

Susan M. Lanterman

When my husband and I considered moving from the suburbs to a nearby college town, we chose our location deliberately. We zeroed in on an old house desperately in need of new life. We found our *Addams Family* Victorian located between a revitalized downtown and a university bursting at the seams. For half a century, the 120-year-old residence had served as a boarding house. Fraternities had invaded stately homes in adjacent neighborhoods—ravaging the integrity of their dwellings with beer pong and balcony beach parties. Our antique abode had remained intact, to a fault. Our mission was to rescue it from becoming just another *Animal House*—only to find that it already was one.

The ink was barely dry on our purchase when we decided to hire our nephew and his college cohorts to demo the interior. Armed with hammers and crowbars, they came prepared to storm the castle. The *Band of Brothers* soon discovered that the perimeter of the house was fortified by ornery groundhogs. Having the advantage of camouflage apparel, militaristic mentalities, and one year of collegiate training, one would have thought our side would be victorious. But at the end of the day their weapons had been hurled down (from the second story) in an effort to scare the beasts away so they could exit the house.

During the renovation, we scoured the interior to find hidden treasure, only to discover four locked freezer chests in the dank basement. This subterranean level was referred to as the backdrop for *Silence of the Lambs*. The fortitude of our macho workforce turned out to be only skin deep. They would brave the basement, when required, solely for reconnaissance missions. One day I was tasked with a soda run to the spare refrigerator in the cellar, when I came nose to nose with a hissing possum on top of the freezer. At the end of our screeching match, my husband evicted the family of six out the bulkhead door.

117

After many *Have a Heart* interventions, we felt we had won the war and reclaimed our turf. But renovations can take on a life of their own, and ours was no exception. Our furry foes had stepped it up a notch, recapturing previously acquired footholds. As quickly as we barricaded entryways, the squirrels and groundhogs chewed through them.

Like a scene out of *The Haunting*, we heard creaks, squeaks, and scurrying throughout the house. Braving the nether regions of the house was now assigned to my braver half. "Your mission—should you choose to accept it," I instructed my husband, " is to recover our suitcases from behind enemy lines." Ascending the attic stairs, he was immediately dive-bombed by something. Before he knew it, he was starring in his own version of *The Birds*, dodging an avian barrage that had penetrated the eaves. Grabbing a tennis racket, he bravely retreated his way back downstairs to safety.

After creating a "no fly zone" in the attic using foam insulation, we moved our base of command to the first floor. We installed a sound machine that was supposed to repel pesky animals overnight. Lulled into a false sense of safety, I opened the door to our spice cabinet one evening and came face to face with a twitching squirrel. The thought of chasing this critter throughout the house was unbearable. I would surrender the job to a professional.

"Who ya gonna call?" my husband queried. Perusal of the yellow pages produced many experts in the business of extermination. I closed my eyes and picked one. Darrell and his slightly intoxicated cousin Darrell soon appeared to rescue us from our standoff. But, alas, *Ghostbusters* they weren't. Armed with fishing nets and a cage, they contemplated the situation while I observed from my perch on the top step above the kitchen. After an hour of futile pursuit, they surrendered to the vermin and left empty-handed—except for the $100 house call. We opened the doors to the spice cabinet and hoped our furry friend would exit up the chimney, from whence he came.

When we purchased our house on the party side of town, we never imaged we would be entertaining such rowdy nightlife within our doors. But our recurring *Nightmare on Elm*

Street continued to play out, featuring infestations of termites, carpenter bees, ants, and mice.

In the end, our acquisition provided a valuable lesson of eminent domain—with a never-ending loop of *Animal Kingdom*.

Nana's Arm

Jean Lancaster

(Second Place Nonfiction, Virginia Writers Club 2014 Summer Shorts Writing Contest)

Ever since Nana was a little girl of three, she had only one arm. My dad, her youngest son, drove our family of six every summer to visit her when she stayed with her elderly sisters in Warm Springs in western Virginia. Along the way, we passed through the small town of Goshen. At that point, Daddy always pointed his arm out the car window and said, "Look, that's where your grandma's arm is buried."

As the eldest daughter and the tallest for looking out the car window, I never knew exactly where or what he was pointing at among the old clapboard houses over to the left. There was no church or stone-walled graveyard that I could see as we whooshed past. Maybe he drove faster because he was afraid we would see a small soiled white cross, forlorn and neglected, under a weeping willow tree. He must have thought that all of us children would begin to sob. Instead, we were in awe and wondered what this meant. Nana was no different than any other grandmother in our eyes.

When Nana was about ten, her father moved their family from Goshen to Warm Springs in Bath County. He was a country doctor, who visited his patients on horseback and carried his medical supplies in a double-pouch, leather saddlebag that lay over his horse's haunches. The family lived in a large farmhouse on the side of Bonner Mountain that was named in his honor.

In 1915, when she was twenty-seven, Nana married our grandfather at Maple Grove Farm in nearby Rockingham County. The Bath County newspaper described the celebration of the marriage of Nell and Richard. "The parlor was artistically decorated in mountain laurel and potted plants, the ceremony taking place under a canopy of spruce arranged in one corner of the room." The bride was "gowned in a blue traveling suit with hat and gloves to match and she carried a shower bouquet of bride's roses." Her older sister, as matron-of-honor, "wore a gown of white lace and carried Kilarney roses." Nana's younger sisters were maids of honor and "wore dainty frocks of white mull and carried pink sweet peas." Her niece presented the wedding ring in "the bloom of a pink rose."

Following the ceremony, "a bountiful dinner was served the bridal party and guests." When they left the wedding festivities, the newly married couple carried "with them the best wishes of a host of friends in this section where the bride has spent her life and where she is deservedly popular."

Nana and Papa settled in Rockingham and later at Merry Oak farm at Gum Springs in Louisa County. Daddy took me to stay with them when I was two years old, while Momma gave birth to my little brother. At that age I must have followed Nana around every day while she checked on her sheep, cut roses for the vases, and brought in firewood for the stove from the woodshed. All these farm tasks must have been much more difficult with only one arm.

In the kitchen she wrapped her one arm around me to set me up on a stool in the mornings to watch her roll and knead the dough for the biscuits. A pitcher of fresh buttermilk always sat on the counter with a glass poured for me.

My brother and I stayed at Merry Oak two years later when my sister was born and during the birth of my youngest brother. While I was there, Nana taught me to play a one-handed duet of "Chopsticks" on the old upright piano in the living room.

When I was older, I became more aware of the scents and images of Merry Oak. In the mornings, salty bacon was still warm on the white-enameled wood stove Nana cooked with ever since my father was a child. In the deep sink was a metal colander of fresh-picked blackberries with morning dew on their bubbled surfaces. Anchoring the center of the room was an oval oak table with its mixture of ladder-back, upholstered, and round-backed Windsor chairs. They reminded me of all the cousins, aunts, and uncles who dined there on Sundays after church at Providence Church.

In the living room, I smelled the comforting fragrance of

the lilac hedge that surrounded the front lawn and floated through the open windows of the two-century-old farmhouse. Nana would sell the blossoms each year. They would be packed in crates and sent off on the train to New York florists. The perfume of the purple wisteria that covered lattice on the side porch glided through the air when Nana and I sat on the porch swing.

Although I never saw Nana with a canvas, oil paint, or brushes, her paintings hung on the walls of the living room and bedrooms. Since she studied art at Randolph-Macon Women's College, Papa and my young father gave her a paint set one Christmas. When her children were almost grown, she started painting again.

My favorite painting was a ruby red cardinal on a branch of a blooming dogwood tree. Another painting was of two silvery fish on a pewter platter. This still life looked like a William Merritt Chase masterpiece. She even painted a small watercolor of a nude woman at the edge of a French lake that was a copy of the infamous and controversial *September Morn* painting by Paul Chabas.

Did Nana have a bit of spunk inside her one-armed anatomy? I thought that was true. Daddy often told the story of how he and his two brothers were helping to dig a new well. Even Nana agreed to be lowered down in the bucket tied to a rope to help bring up the Virginia red clay from the bottom of the hole.

At night Nana would read stories to my siblings, our cousins, and me. We all sat with her on top of her and Papa's tall walnut frame bed. Usually, I was restless and fidgety. She paused in the story to ask if I had "ants in my pants," which truly embarrassed me. As I squirmed even more, I noticed the wink of her eye that softened the admonishment.

We grandchildren never asked Nana about her missing arm. The only explanation we ever had from Daddy was that she lost her arm when she was a child. She, her brothers, and her sisters were playing at rolling over a water barrel turned on its side. It seemed that Nana hurt her arm and it never healed. Her father studied surgery at the University of Virginia Medical School in 1882 and 1883. He had the skills, tools, and the unfortunate task of amputating his young daughter's arm at the shoulder.

As far as I know, Nana never wore a prosthetic arm. Once, though, I happened to see her shoulder when she was dressing and still in her white cotton slip. That part of her shoulder looked like a soft rose, waiting to curl open.

Traveling recently to Warm Springs with my sister and brother for a weekend at the Gristmill Inn, we crossed over the bridge at Goshen. Since I was the eldest, it was my responsibility to point to the left and say, "Look, that's where grandma's arm is buried."

The Price of a Pig

Erin Newton Wells

(First place nonfiction, Blue Ridge Writers VWC, 2014)

It shocked him to hear himself called old. Two women on their break stood by the door of a fried pie factory on the outskirts of our neighborhood. He was on one of the regular walks for his health, swinging along at a reasonable pace in the rolling gait caused by one leg being just a bit shorter.

"See that ol man?" the first woman said to the other. "He go by here evvyday."

In his usual good humor, my father reported the observation to us, trying to see it from the woman's point of view and treating it with his customary charity. But I could tell it puzzled him and that he had not thought of himself in this way before. None of us did. He seemed always the tall, blue-eyed twin of the Duke of Windsor in his earlier days, the same light-brown sweep of hair, the elegant, flexible body. And he had that same gentle smile, with the questioning brow. He was not old. But it was all right if the pie woman wanted to think so.

The times in which I grew up were still favorable to walkers. We were a relatively small community in Beaumont, Texas, still centered in our neighborhoods, without the commercial and residential sprawl that would occur later. Our family did not own a car for many years, so anything in the area was reached by walking. We walked to school and to the corner grocers and to the houses of our friends. For something too far, like going downtown where my father worked as chief accountant at the post office, we rode the city bus. These were big white and yellow affairs with open windows, no air-conditioning yet, and clouds of nauseating fumes.

Dressed in suit and hat, my father would walk in the morning to the end of the block and around the corner, past Cireo's grocery, to the Royal Street bus stop. He returned by the same route at the end of the day. When I was little, I waited until he rounded the corner, with that Duke of Windsor smile. Then I ran all the way to meet him, and the two of us walked home. In summer, his jacket was over his shoulder, and his white shirt sleeves were rolled up in the humid Gulf air. His hat was light straw. In winter, the jacket was on, and he wore a felt fedora. He smelled of cold air and of the post office, a mix of federal granite, letters, and stamps.

A mysterious medical event happened involving my father when I was still young. It was not explained to me, and I can only piece together what it might have been. Probably it is what initiated the more vigorous walking campaign in evenings after work and on weekends. I recall that my father had to be in the hospital a few days, that his skin turned yellow from jaundice, and that he was put on a strict diet for a while. Was it an infection or malfunction of the liver? I don't know and was too young to know to ask. My mother cooked good meals that had no fat. When he was better, he began the walks for his health, such as the one that, much later, took him past the pie factory.

Often I accompanied him on these rounds of the neighborhood. They were a source of great enjoyment to both of us and of valuable lessons for me, although he never intentionally presented it that way. What I learned came from him aslant by observing what he did and how he said it. More likely than not, it was in just one tiny passing expression on his face, which he did not know was seen. These unintended lessons were about kindness, about trying to see from a point of view other than your own.

On weekends in the autumn, when the heavy air of East Texas finally cooled and turned moderately crisp, we would sometimes drive to wooded places and get out to walk. This, of course, was after we had a car. The first of these was a used black Chevrolet from the 1940s. It was high, rounded, and dignified, with running boards and heavy chrome handles to open the little vent windows, and a source of great pride to the children of the family. We took Sunday drives in this. But the next car, a charcoal gray Plymouth of the 1950s, is the one in which I remember riding with my father on our autumn adventures.

Fall was our favorite time. He and I would stroll and soak up warm sun. It always inspired him to talk about the history of England. Our conversations covered 1066, with the Norman invasion, Battle of Hastings, and Bayeux Tapestry. Or it could be earlier, with the waves of Picts, Scots, and Jutes tumbling through Britain, painting themselves blue with woad and tussling over Hadrian's wall. Or it could be later, the London of Samuel Pepys and his famous diary. My father had a complete copy and read to us from it regularly.

Several autumn weekends stand out in my memory, because we drove to the Southeast Texas State Fairgrounds in our town to take walks in the large shaded area of old trees. We crunched through leaves and acorns. Oak galls that had fallen bobbled out of the way. The smell of pine straw warmed by sun surrounded us. Here were the great exhibit barns for livestock, produce, and crafts, all empty now. One of them housed a few parade floats. Through these rambles my father wove tales of England and the sad injustice that befell Harold, the losing Celts, or the unfortunate citizens of London beset with plague and fire.

One summer, in a fit of needing to blend with my school crowd, I begged to be taken to the fair with a friend, and my father agreed to do so. This was after my grandparents moved in with us, and my grandfather came along. It was his car we were using by then, a Chevrolet with no backseat. My friend and I sat cross legged on the floor, before the era of seat belts.

I didn't really like the fair. It was noisy, hot, crowded, tawdry, so unlike the quiet times I shared there with my father. I went through it because it was what other children did. In this spirit, I asked to have a foot-long hot dog, one of the fair's extravagant items, and my father obliged. My friend chose something more modest, and my grandfather chuckled and waved off the offer of such ridiculous food.

In looking back, I realize that my father assumed I would break the lengthy bun in half and offer part to him. This was well after the earlier health restrictions, and I knew how much he really liked hot dogs. But I was caught up in the invented popular image of myself. With an air of childish bravado, perhaps to impress my friend, I managed to consume the entire thing myself. When I saw his face afterward, that brief glimpse of sadness on it, I sensed what I had done. He never said a word. But I knew that momentarily I completely forgot him, my good, generous father. I had pushed aside those nearly hallowed times we shared in that place, and now I felt miserable. It became an awakening, just that fleeting expression that spoke more deeply than any lecture. I saw that I was capable of thievery and had stolen from him. It had little to do with a fanciful bit of food. It had everything to do with ripping out pieces of the loyalty and love that connected us.

Such occasions may seem trivial, even silly, at first, but they were leading me somewhere important. It took more than one of them, for I was a slow learner. A second instance of this realization, as it turns out, also is associated with food. My father often did the cooking on weekends to give my mother a break. Sunday lunch after church was her province, but weekend breakfast, Saturday lunch, and Sunday evening supper usually fell to him. He would go shopping on Saturday morning for his type of food. We had entered the time of supermarkets, instead of small corner grocers, so this involved the car, sometimes with me along. He would buy wieners, buns, pickles, mustard, sauerkraut, chips, pork 'n beans, a harkening back to his German upbringing. Frequently this fare became our family's Saturday lunch. On the way home, we stopped at Daniel's Bakery for a surprise of cinnamon buns, which stayed in their white, slightly grease-spotted bag atop the refrigerator until after lunch.

On Sunday evenings, he cooked scrambled eggs and bacon, which we ate at the kitchen table while listening to radio broadcasts of *Jack Benny*, *Fibber McGee and Molly*, and *Amos and Andy*. For a time, he and I had an agreement that after these meals he would wash the dishes and I would dry and put them away. It gave us another opportunity for our talks about history, literature, and what we called The Lore, concerning life in his childhood days.

I recall that on one Sunday evening, instead of helping to clear the colorful Fiesta Ware plates and utensils used for our family suppers, I pretended to be lost in thought. I let him clear the table and wash the dishes. I pretended not to see him glance at me once when things began to stack up in the drying rack. I pretended not to see him pick up the dish towel and dry each piece and put it away. But I did see that brief, sad look, just like the one at the fair. He never mentioned it, never admonished me, and I never spoke up to apologize. I don't know why I did it, and it hurt me deeply afterward that, again, I had been so selfish. Like the incident at the fair, it pushed me around another hard corner, scraping away at the wrongness of this difficult thing I needed to learn. I had presumed upon his goodness and had stolen from him, right out in plain sight of both of us.

Every little thing about my father had to do with kindness. I cannot think of any ill will that he bore. He never raised his voice or spoke sharply. He never harmed anything. One day as we set out to make a tour of the neighborhood, we came across a black ant crossing the sidewalk. My father rerouted us, making a wide circle around the ant, so as not to disturb its transit.

"He's going home from work," he said. "His children will be sad if he doesn't get there."

Immediately I understood. The ant was my father. I was the ant child. A whole philosophy was condensed in this small exchange over a very tiny subject. You must become the other thing. You must feel how it feels. That was the source of his great kindness. Harming others was unthinkable.

This carried over even to things that might seem absurd. We were an allergy-prone family, always carrying handkerchiefs and then, later, the great luxury of Kleenex tissues when they appeared in the world. All of us were out for a drive around town, the windows open, I in the backseat with an arm resting on the window edge. The Kleenex in my hand flew out of the car.

"The poor Kleenex," said my father, jokingly.

And yet I wondered if even the Kleenex had someone at home waiting. I wanted to go back and retrieve it from the roadside, but we couldn't. From then on, I was more careful on these drives. It was an outstanding deterrent to littering, before the days when people were much concerned with it.

Everything deserved to be considered equally, no matter how small. There was, for example, no hierarchy of importance for people in my father's eyes. He was kind to the little ones of the town. We found out about this from time to time, but never from him. He made a point of remembering names and greeted everyone. This included the clerks, cashiers, cafeteria workers at the Piccadilly, where he had his coffee break and lunch, and the shoeshine man at the stand in front of the Hotel Beaumont. He kept a list of their birthdays and made sure they received a card each year. He built an invisible network of simple kindnesses throughout the town. They spoke of him as though he were a saint, that it was unusual to be treated this way.

He also made sure to buy things from the blind man and his blind wife who ran a small concession with newspapers, magazines, and candy bars in the post office lobby. Each Friday evening we could expect to be given a comic book, still smelling of the post office, from the blind man's stand. There was one for each of us. My sister, the oldest, got *Illustrated Classics*. My brother got *Donald Duck*. I, the youngest, had *Little Lulu*. I used to think this was done just as a nice surprise for us. But later I realized it was for the blind man, too. Everyone was going home from work to children, so to speak. Everyone was valued. My father would no more steal a person's self-worth than he would steal their money.

Our walking routes would change over periods of time, but one that repeated frequently when I was younger took us all the way to Johnson's Florist. It passed by the corner building, which, at a future date, the fried pie industry would occupy. It seemed like such a long way, but I was eager to reach the florist shop, where we could look in the large, plateglass window at the beautiful seasonal displays. The best was at Christmas, with animated figures of Mr. and Mrs. Santa dressed in deep, red velvet and bowing courteously to each other and to us.

The Easter window was also enchanting, with a great, kindly rabbit moving his head and arms jerkily over hundreds of large, pastel eggs. It was during the Easter season that I discovered the pig. Next to the florist was a lovely yard. It was shady and full of shrubbery and flowers. I happened to look down at the edge of a flower bed that fronted the sidewalk and saw something pale pink. I stooped to probe this with my fingers and pulled from the dirt a small porcelain pig, not more than two inches long. It was old and soiled, the shiny finish dulled and crazed, probably long abandoned by a child or, perhaps, a gardener making a miniature scene. I wanted it.

This presented a dilemma. I knew I should not take things that belonged to another. My father saw the great and immediate need I had for this tiny creature. After a moment he reached in his pocket and brought out a few coins, which he stared at, putting all but one aside, a quarter. He bent down and pushed the coin into the dirt beside the pig. It was a fair exchange. This now made it all right for me to have it. We had paid for it.

But more was involved here. The coin chosen was not a penny or a nickel, or even a dime, but a whole quarter, which had value then. It was the day when a penny rolled five gumballs out of a machine, and a five-and-ten-cent store was actually a place where useful things could be purchased for those amounts. A quarter was more than my father spent on his coffee break or a bus ride. It was big money to me, and to him. He put himself where I was. He gave worth to my need. I kept the pig for years, but it slipped away, perhaps for another child to find and for which an observant father must now pay five dollars, at least.

He never lost touch with his childhood, and that is what made him so understanding of us. He had a wise innocence with which he swept the scenery aside and got to the heart of who we really were. He never grew old. His face never lost its youthfulness, although eventually it was Parkinson's that slowed him down. It stiffened his body so that he could only shuffle slowly, and then not even that. The last time I saw him, he was lying in a bed, unable to move. He had a tube in his throat to help him breathe and could not speak. But his eyes could, and his eyes loved me.

He continued to be kind to the attendants, to everyone, showing it in whatever way he could. He did not want to be a trouble for others. He probably would have sent cards to them, if he were able. I'm guessing he followed up years earlier with those two women at the pie factory and handed them remembrances on their birthdays, pushing quarters into the earth wherever he saw value.

My Dad's Last Gun

Jody Hobbs Hesler

(Second place nonfiction, Blue Ridge Writers VWC, 2014)

It wasn't when my father's M.S. required him to use Canadian crutches in order to walk that he got rid of his last gun. It wasn't after the fall that dislocated his hip and kept him in a rehab hospital for weeks on end. It wasn't because of the uncontrollable muscle spasms brought on by the M.S. And, even after he was in a wheelchair, for years his friends somehow dragged him and his chair into deer blinds so he could hunt with them. It wasn't until after the summer I studied abroad during college that he got rid of his last gun.

A man of few cautions, my dad crashed so many cars, under the influence and otherwise, that no company in Virginia would cover him. He had to get his car insurance out of Pennsylvania. On a windy Fourth of July, he was the one to suggest that my nine- or ten-year-old brother lean over the match to keep it lit long enough to light the firework that blew up in my brother's face, searing off all his eyebrows and eyelashes, leaving him with a small horseshoe-shaped scar at the bridge of his nose that lasted for years, and sealing his eyelids shut. During several visits and under special lights that made the gunpowder phosphoresce, the eye doctor lifted glowing chunks from his eyes until they were clean. My dad stored his stockpile of illegal fireworks under the bed I slept in when we visited.

I never saw guns around my father's house, but I knew he hunted. I also knew he had accidentally left one, loaded, in his luggage on a trip to Hawaii with my mom before their divorce. If he hadn't funded my study abroad trip the summer of 1988, though, I would not have known he still kept a gun handy and wouldn't have guessed why he would choose that time to give it up.

My father was a Realtor and went in and out of money like other people went in and out of the rain. For a while he was also involved in some kind of business "selling tents to the

Arabs," as he put it, which required numerous trips to England when I was a child. He drove Mercedes Benz convertibles or 1960 limousines until he wrecked them and bought the next car.

He didn't spend his money on his kids. He took me clothes shopping twice in my life and sent child support late as often as he sent it at all. The government excused him from all financial obligations to his family when he filed for disability. Even while he collected disability, though, he continued to manage a company he co-owned without reporting his earnings to the government.

All he paid toward college for my brother or me was the $800 he had saved for my brother (zero for me, because I was a girl). With it, my brother bought the best car $800 could get—a decrepit station wagon that wouldn't go faster than 35 mph. Its fabric ceiling hung down and bounced on your head. The whole car stunk of mildew.

I paid for my own books and incidental expenses at college from money I saved working summers and Christmases. My mother paid everything else. When I mentioned a study abroad poster I'd seen to my father over the phone, I was making conversation. It never occurred to me he might offer to send me abroad for summer study.

When he did, I combined gratitude with skepticism. "This is really amazing," I'd tell him, "but if you can't pay for all of it, please don't pay for any of it. I can't afford to go on my own." The time after my final exams and before the trip was not long enough for me to earn the money I would need to cover even airfare, let alone tuition, books for my courses, and lunches the program did not include. So when I applied to study at Cambridge University for the summer of 1988, I also applied for a study abroad scholarship. Both my dad and I would have felt more comfortable if he didn't have to pay for everything. I was runner up.

I never counted on the trip as a sure thing until I was on board the plane. And even then, the matter wasn't settled. The weekend before my final exams, only about three weeks before I would leave for my trip, my father called me. "I sent off the tuition for that program," he said. "But I won't be able to pay for the rest after all."

I wasn't too surprised to learn the trip was off. "You can go ahead and cancel the check," I told him. "If you still want to spend that money for me, maybe you could get me a car or something."

After my exams, my father called me back and told me the trip was on again. A fiancée of his I never met convinced him to follow through on the promise he had made to me. He told me he would be able to send half of what I needed at the beginning of the trip, but, because of some kind of financial hiccup he didn't explain, the rest would have to come later. I boarded the plane to England, unsure if I would have enough money to pay for my lunches all the way through.

Every day I went to the American Express office to ask about the pending wire transfer from my dad. Some of my books were less expensive than I had figured, which bought me a little extra time. The money I made working two jobs those few weeks before the trip bought me a little more time, though I had planned to use that to buy books for my fall semester.

Three weeks into my six-week program, the balance of the money finally arrived. I never missed a meal.

I hadn't imagined such an extravagant opportunity. Cambridge dons were among our teachers. We learned about modern British poetry and the transit of European cultures to America in Colonial times. We took day trips to see Royal Shakespeare Company productions in London and to tour East Anglian medieval abbeys. We nodded hello to Stephen Hawking, who was a fellow at Gonville and Caius, the Cambridge University college that hosted our program. We discovered scones with jam and cream, darts, pubs, lagers and lime, punting the Cam, and more. I accepted my dad's money hang-ups as nothing more than his initials on the trip.

Some months after I came home, my father told me over the phone about what had caused the money troubles. To explain, I need to introduce "Ian" and "Betsy."

Ian was a long-time friend of my dad. Born into a wealthy family, Ian suffered from spinobiphida, which kept him in a wheelchair until, by sheer determination, he learned to walk at seventeen. A year later, the uncle who raised him died. He had spent every penny of the family fortune and left Ian penniless.

Betsy was born dirt poor. Her mother believed she was the queen of England and held court regularly in the lobby of the Battletowne Inn to greet her subjects. When Betsy joined my mother for tea before my parents' divorce, she added spoonful after spoonful of sugar into her cup because her family hadn't had the luxury of sugar when she was growing up.

Ian and Betsy fell in love and married. They had a farmhouse on a Virginia mountainside, with four children, seventeen cats, and a pet deer who ate from the table. Ian landed a corporate job, and things went along fine until he began embezzling—large enough sums of money that the feds stayed on his trail until a few weeks shy of the seven-year statute of limitations, when they finally nabbed him outside a hotel in Ocean City, Maryland. Ian spent time in federal prison. When he got out, he needed to borrow some money.

So he borrowed $10,000 from my father.

Later, Ian drove up to my dad's house in a brand new BMW to tell him he wouldn't be able to pay him back, and that is why my father nearly canceled my trip to England.

"You loaned him money? A convicted embezzler?" I said.

"He was my friend for years."

"So loan him your car. Not ten thousand bucks!"

My dad was so angry, he was afraid what would happen if Ian visited again. So he took his gun apart, melted down the individual pieces, and threw them away so no one could use it again.

And that was my dad's last gun.

Light in the Forest

Phyllis R. Koch-Sheras

(Third place nonfiction, Blue Ridge Writers VWC, 2014)

What an unusual situation, these two middle-aged women—one an American Jew, the other a German Christian—standing there in the middle of the ski lodge, hugging and crying. To this day, it still moves me to think about it.

The Jewish woman was me almost three decades ago. The German woman was my old friend and colleague, Barbara, who I had not seen in nearly fifteen years.

It's a beautiful spring day in Switzerland, where I am visiting her and her husband for a few days while on some European travels. On that particular day, Barbara and I decide to go cross-country skiing.

"I was hoping to ski while I was here," I tell her. "I love it, and I hardly ever get to do any real skiing outside of the small hills of Virginia," I tell her. It is a beautiful ride through densely wooded areas to the ski area. "What a beautiful forest," I remark.

"Yes," Barbara says, "this is the Black Forest."

I immediately feel a shudder, since my first association, as a Jew, is to Jewish people escaping through that forest during the Holocaust. "Well, at least we're still in Switzerland, not Germany," I think. I keep my thoughts to myself and try to ignore them as we put on our skis and hit the trail.

There is still a chill in the air, but the sky is bright and clear. The snow is sparkling in the sunshine through the trees. Barbara knows the terrain and leads the way. "We have now crossed into the German part of the forest," she yells back at me. I gasp in surprise, my dear deceased father's words ringing in my ears: "I will never set foot in Germany as long as I live, and I don't want my family going there either." I immediately lose my balance and fall flat on my face. My nose is bleeding, and I lay crumpled on the ground. I look up and see blood all over the snow. Suddenly, I start trembling and feel faint. Visions of being chased through the forest by the Gestapo flood over me. "Oh, no!" I cry, tears streaming down my face.

"Are you all right, Phyllis?" she says, as she comes back for me. I just keep crying and shaking. She takes me back to the lodge, sits me down in a comfortable chair, and cleans my wounds. "Would you like me to do some healing massage for your nose?" she asks.

She seems confident and relaxed, and I whisper, "Yes, please."

After a short time, the swelling has gone down, and I begin to feel less pain and panic. I tell Barbara about my associations and flashback, and she starts telling me about her family history. We had never discussed any of this before.

"I knew you were Jewish," she tells me. "I was always reluctant to tell you about my past. Would you like to hear about it now?"

"Yes, I would."

"My father had been in the Nazi army. He and our family suffered terribly after the war from penalties and recriminations by the Allied forces. Both my parents lost their jobs, and my father was interrogated relentlessly by the Allied forces."

"I had no idea. I am so sorry you went through all that." I go over to Barbara, and we stand together, hugging and crying for several minutes. In that moment, feelings of compassion for both her and my father blend together in a confusing rush.

I put this incident in the back of my mind until last year, when I am on a Tibetan Buddhist spiritual retreat. During a meditation practice, the leader asks, "What might be blocking the experience of joy in your life?" Suddenly, I start shaking with fear and anger, and tears start flowing uncontrollably down my face. An overwhelming sense of despair comes over me.

"I am having an experience of being trapped and captured by the Gestapo in the Black Forest," I am finally able to tell the group. The leader suggests that I chant a mantra that involves the healing power of fire. I am unable to do it, as it brings up visions of the gas chambers during the Holocaust.

"Would you like the group to do chanting and breathing together with you," I hear the group leader ask me.

"Yes, please." I allow the healing sounds and connection with the group to flow through me. My tears, fear, and anger begin to dissipate, and I am able to hear sharing from the group members.

"This is helping me deal with feelings about my ancestors being held in Japanese internment camps here in the U.S. during WWII," one Asian woman says to the group. "I am so glad this came up and that you shared this with us."

That night, after our last session, a friend asks me to go for a walk on the path near the retreat center. The woods on the path are dark and dense. It is a beautiful night, but I feel uneasy and fearful. "Oh, let's do it," I say after thinking about it. I follow him, feeling safe and protected. The next night at the retreat, I even took a walk into the woods by myself. There was a full moon, and the moonlight inspired me. When I started to feel afraid, I chanted some prayers and felt my confidence return. I enjoyed the walk and felt proud of myself for doing it.

Interestingly enough, the very next day after the retreat, I was seeing one of my therapy clients of German heritage, who shared some interesting information about his history. "My great uncle had been one of Hitler's right-hand men. I still feel tremendous guilt about that and a lot of anger about the rough treatment my family endured from the Allies after the war. My aunt was raped by some of the soldiers, and she never got over that."

His sharing touched my heart, and instead of the wall I might have put up in the past, I felt deep compassion for him, for my friend Barbara, and for all victims of war. Other thoughts and questions have come up for me since then about the Holocaust and the anger and shame I still feel about that time. "How could the world stand by for so long and let this happen? How could the Jews let this happen to themselves? How do I deal with my guilt about me and members of my family surviving while so many others perished?"

I was also able to identify a pervasive pattern of suffering in other areas of my life, both personally and professionally, that has depleted my power and confidence. I have focused several meditation practices on that pattern and have experienced feeling stronger in all areas of my life, including as a writer,

137

which has enabled me to write about this experience. I can risk standing out and being successful now without the fear of drawing jealousy or condemnation, such as with the Nazis. Making these connections has freed me up to be more open, compassionate, and honest with people in my life. I can tell my husband when I am angry with him without fear of reprisals. I can have compassion for my sister, even when she is expressing disappointment and anger toward me.

I continue to do meditation practices to dissipate my anger, guilt, and grief and am beginning to sense a lifting of that trauma from the past that blocked my fully experiencing joy and love in my life. We never know where the opportunity or door to joy may present itself. Who thought that, for me, it would be through a fall while skiing in the Black Forest? In fact, the whole experience turned out to be a valuable gift for me—and hopefully can be for others as well who may suffer from various forms of generational trauma: slaves and slave owners, Jews and Germans, Japanese in internment camps, Native Americans, and on and on.

Fortunately, it is possible to resolve generational trauma. That was definitely the case for one of my clients whose grandparents were slave owners. I was so impressed with how he resolved his anger at them and his parents for not addressing the racism that was the norm in their culture. Ultimately, he was able to grieve the sadness underlying his history and forgive his parents for not seeking to change the racial inequality they lived in. He was able to write a letter to his mother (his father was deceased) and then talk with her honestly and respectfully about all of this. The letter ended with the affirmation that "I trust that . . . I will achieve peace and compassion that comes with acknowledgement, acceptance and respect of others, as well as myself." He completed therapy promising to use his past as an opportunity to appreciate diversity and the changes inherent in every generation.

I believe that by coming together and sharing—survivors and perpetrators alike—more reconciliation, completion, and transformation can take place. My deepest desire is that this happens in our lifetime. Then there can truly be light in the forest.

My Father's World

Leonard Tuchyner

The old oak table that usually brought our family together at suppertime was now an impregnable barrier separating my father and me. He didn't like what I was saying.

I was fifteen and desperately trying to understand the world that I had somehow been dumped in. I didn't know why I was here. Why anyone was here. Why was Here . . . here? In other words, "What's it all about, Alfie?" It terrified me to consider the possibility that there was no 'Why'. Maybe there was just some meaningless cosmic accident with no purpose, and when my brain would cut off, so would I.

"Dad, why do I have to take the school bus? There are a lot of other ways I could get there."

"Because that's what everybody else in St. Petersburg does."

"That's not true. Most of my friends take a car or a scooter."

"You don't have a car or a scooter."

"Yeah, I know that, Dad," I said, spreading the sarcasm dangerously thick. "But I have a bike."

"It's too far for a bike."

"Why's that?"

"Because it is."

"You don't have any basis for saying that." I was tempted to say, "You don't know what you're talking about," but it didn't seem like a good day to die. Nevertheless, I could tell my father was getting frustrated.

This was not an argument about whether I had to ride the school bus. In fact, unbeknownst to my parents, I was already getting to school by hitchhiking. No, this was a battle against arbitrary absolutes, better known as Authority.

I knew we were headed for loud voices, so I went full speed ahead. "You can't say that anything IS." I should have said, "*We* can't know," but I was going after him.

139

"What are you talking about? You're not making any sense." He had a slightly amused look on his face. It was the look of someone witnessing a seventy-pound weakling trying to pick a fight with him. That infuriated me.

"This table doesn't exist," I blurted out.

"That's stupid." The amusement was starting to darken.

"I'm reading a book on Buddhism, and it says everything is illusion. They call it Maya."

He stared at me in angry disbelief. "This table is real."

"It's only real because you think it is."

Without warning, he burst out of his chair. smote the table top with both fists, and shouted, "There. Is that real enough?" It was not a question. It was a very convincing point. Then he stormed out of the dining room.

I went outside to the back of our house, climbed the TV aerial pole, and hung out on the roof. Sometimes I conjured up lofty thoughts up there. Sometimes I remembered things.

My father was a traditionalist, and none of that had to do with religion. To him, life was responsibility. You worked hard and owned a house with nice furniture that showed you were a good provider. He was as solid as that oak table. I felt secure in his steadiness, and I never had to guess what to expect from him.

The Snow Ride

I remember a day when I was about four or five, when snow covered the ground. In those days near the end of World War Two, snow stayed, relatively unmolested, in the streets. Except on major thoroughfares, the traffic was light, and all the old cars wore chains that made a wonderful chinking sound. I was walking along the curb of a snowy street, holding my father's hand. In his other hand, he dragged a sled by its tether.

"Where we goin', Daddy?"

"Irvington Park."

"Why?"

"You'll see."

So I trudged along the best I could, all bundled up with too much clothing, including boots that took my mother an eternity to get me into. Of course, I whined during the entire dressing routine.

"We gonna go up the hill, Daddy?"

"Yes."

"Why?"

"You'll see."

The hill was a long, steep, winding path about six feet wide. When we got there, older boys were sliding down, head first, on their sleds. It looked scary.

"I don't wanna, Daddy."

He didn't say anything, but kept going up the side of the path until we reached the flat spot at the top. I had no choice but to keep up. There kids waited their turn to bellywop down the grade. I thought my father might go down by himself and leave me at the summit waiting for him. I certainly wasn't going to hang on piggyback while he ran and dived headfirst down the slope, with that contraption under us. I didn't know the word for suicide, but I got the concept.

When it was our turn, he gently lay, stomach down, on the slider.

"Now, lie down on top of me."

"Why?"

"Just do it." This was not a discussion. It was an order. So I did what I was told.

He started using his arms and hands to move the sled off the flat starting point, and we began sliding, as gravity took over.

"I'm falling, Daddy."

"No you're not." Who was I to argue with him?

He steered us around the curves, and by the time we went into a snow bank at the end of the run, I was laughing, even as I tumbled into the bank. After that, I couldn't get enough.

Now the thing was that holding on to him gave me some sense of security, once I knew there was no way out. That's what he was all about—security. He married a woman whose insatiable need for assurance was a proper vessel that gave his life purpose. It was a fine kettle of fish in which to grow up. My mother's conviction that Chicken Little was correct and the sky was really falling was balanced by my father's assurance that he could hold it up. The world might be going to hell in a hand basket, but if I rode on my father's shoulders, I might not be burnt. Notice the key phrase "might not."

Anyway, after that sleigh ride experience, I never saw him slide again. He had done his job well, and I now had a new sustaining interest to get me through long snowy winters.

Kite Flying

That Spring I again found myself in tow toward Irvington Park.

"Daddy, is that really gonna fly?" The hope and wonder in my voice, I'm sure, was unmistakable.

"That's what kites do."

"Do you throw it?" By this time I had seen paper airplanes glide and thought the phenomenon was the coolest thing since puppies.

"When we get to the park, I'll put it together, and you'll see."

At that point I was trying to drag him to go faster. This was the most exciting thing I had ever heard of, and I had no doubt that that colorful piece of paper wrapped around two sticks was somehow going to take off and fly like a bird.

After eons, we finally arrived.

"Hurry up, Daddy."

"Hold your horses. This may take some time."

"How much time, Daddy?"

"I'll let you know when it's ready."

I jumped impatiently from one foot to the other, as he unfolded the beautiful triangle of blue kite, the prettiest blue I'd ever seen. I watched intently as he stretched it between two slotted sticks of wood, fashioned a bridle, and tied an endlessly long ball of string to it.

"Will it fly now, Daddy? Will you make it fly?"

He didn't say anything but went to one end of the field and started running. The kite followed behind on a short tether, acting like a crazed squirrel, jumping from side to side in every direction except up. My dad ran all the way across the field several times, as I watched with a growing sense of profound disappointment. Oh, how I wanted that kite to fly. I needed it to defy gravity and take my soul to freedom. I dared not give up that hope and dream.

"Let's try something else," he said, undaunted. "You hold the kite up like this." He demonstrated. "I'll let out the string, and when I tell you, let go."

He walked away about thirty yards and yelled, "Let go!" I felt the tether pull before it registered on me that I was supposed to release my grip. He came walking back, obviously irritated.

"Didn't you hear me say to let go?"

"I'm sorry. I didn't mean not to let go."

"OK, let's try it again."

He walked away once more and picked up the ball of twine lying where he left it. At that point I let go, in anticipation, before he told me to.

"I didn't tell you to let go," he screamed. "Pick up the kite and don't let go until I tell you to, this time." I think it is a credit to him that he was not cursing by then. Actually, I don't remember hearing him use four-letter words, ever.

The third time I got it right, and he took off running down the field. The kite went up a little bit, but it didn't seem to have its heart in it and promptly fell listlessly to earth when my father ran out of field.

About that time, a grown-up bystander walked over to my father and told him what he was doing wrong. He hadn't bowed the cross bar. After that, the kite found its wings.

My reactions were conflicted. My father had failed, and yet he hadn't. He managed to find the resources to fulfill my desires, but he did not know how to fly. He was earthbound. I felt shame for Dad needing someone else's father to help him, but my joy in the freedom of flight soared. I flew kites for the rest of my life. But never again with my dad. He had done his job and was through with it. Flying was for children.

I find it baffling that when my father laughed, he laughed like a child. He didn't allow himself children's' games, but his inner child came out in his laughter and zany jokes. Go figure. Someday I'll write about that conundrum.

The Sailboat Affair

Two blocks from our rented duplex apartment was a minimalist shopping area. In the nineteen-forties, these were very common in pre-suburbia America. Though I couldn't have been more than five or six, I was allowed to roam free as a neighborhood dog. In those days, this was the practice, and thank God for that. I passed a store window once while wandering the extended neighborhood and was captured by the sight of a little kid-sized sailboat. It should not be a surprise to the reader, by this time, that I was enthralled. I was possessed by a fundamental need that seemed to mirror my soul's essence. Although I had as much avarice as any kid my age, this want was so much more intense than my normal greed; it would be like comparing a firecracker to an atomic bomb. My life depended on owning it. I was willing to risk anything. It was greater than Ralphie's desire for a BB gun in *A Christmas Story*. I also knew I would get it. That was preordained. I rushed home to ask my parents to buy it for me. This was very atypical. The fact that they were entertaining guests and that my intrusion would be an embarrassment didn't matter. In fact, it played to my advantage. They wouldn't kill me in front of their guests.

I walked into the living room, feigning meekness. "Daddy, will you buy me a sailboat that I saw at the store?"

"Is it your birthday?"

"No, Daddy."

"Is it Chanukah?"

"No, Daddy"

"Then you can't have it. If you still want it when the occasion arises, we'll consider it."

The company smiled and looked at me quizzically.

"Please, please, please!" I knew this wouldn't do it, but it was only the opening salvo. My parents didn't dare show the anger they must have been feeling.

I sniffled, made mewing sounds like a plaintive kitten, and left the room like I'd just lost my best friend.

Fifteen minutes later was time for round two. Without preamble, "Please, please. I'll never ask for anything else again. Please."

"I said no. Now stop interrupting us."

The guests' glances were switching back and forth between me and my parents, as though they were watching a tennis match, with money down on their favorite.

I left the room again but increased the level of drama concerning my message of broken-heartedness. That was the end of round two.

Round three: This time I was determined to stay and fight, no matter what. My father got the message. He either had to break my neck or give ground. The trick was to do it without losing face. "We'll talk about it if you'll go away."

"Boy-oh-boy!"

"I said we'll talk about it, not that we'll buy it for you."

But I knew better. I got a pretty good dressing down when the company left, but I also got my sailboat.

The only connection I can remember that my father ever had with boats was after he retired and took my mother on a cruise. That's a totally different species from a sailing vessel. One flies on the wind, with sails for wings, and the other is a floating powered box that is designed to insulate the travelers from the sea. Remember, my father did not know how to fly, nor was he interested in flying. But he could tell that it was deeply, if unexplainably, important to me.

As it turned out, the little wooden sailboat would not sail. It turned on its side and stayed there as soon as a puff of wind touched its sail. It needed to be stabilized. My dad was an expert in stability. He kept adding weights to its keel until it was so bottom-heavy that it would right itself like a weighted clown balloon. Having done that, he tied a string around my wrist that attached me to the boat so it wouldn't float or be blown away. It was so safe and predictable I quickly lost interest. But, as an adult, when I had the chance, I went sailing in real sailboats whenever I could. I owned and built them.

My father could rarely be coaxed to even wade in water. He drove us to the beaches, sat around with the sunbathers for a little while, or just went home, to pick us up when it was time to go home, if we were vacationing. I don't even know for sure that he could swim. I had a dread of water over my head for a major part of my childhood, but I overcame that fear. When I did, I became foolhardy and nearly drowned on more than two occasions. Swimming, particularly underwater, was a little like flying.

My obsession with escaping gravity was, and is, a metaphysical and spiritual quest. I was, and am, desperate to know that my existence supersedes the mundane—that after my bones and brain stop functioning, it simply means my tether will have been severed from the physical world.

My Father's Death

Dad lived to ninety-two and worked into his seventies. Gradually, his body fell to pieces, and he spent his latter years in a wheelchair. Several operations on his back did little to slow his crippling. He became so deaf that it was impossible to communicate with him via telephone, and most of his generation knew little to nothing about computers. In his last days, while in a nursing home, I communicated with him by typing on a computer. His eyes were perfectly clear, as was his mind.

"Dad, are you afraid of dying?" I wrote.

In a voice that was as strong as if he were in his forties, he answered, "No."

"Do you think there is anything after this life?"

"No."

"Doesn't that bother you?"

"Why should it? I've had enough of life."

"Do you think life has a purpose?"

"Yes, of course it does."

"If you get turned off like a lightbulb, what purpose could life have?"

"You take care of your family. You live honestly and take pleasure where you can."

This was, in many ways, the same discussion we had across the oak table. The only thing real to him was what he could know by his senses. There was no such thing as spirit or

146

anything else that did not give the impression of three-dimensional existence. It still seemed to upset him to consider an alternative. I regret not asking him if there was a God. But I think he would have considered the question irrelevant.

"Dad, how do you feel?"

"I feel so tired that it is the worst pain that you could possibly imagine."

My father died of heart failure in a nursing home. The night he died, the night nurse said he kept saying over and over again, "Take me, take me, take me."

She didn't know if he was awake or sleeping. I think she interpreted his words to mean that he was praying to God to take him to Heaven. I would like to believe that he was beseeching someone or something. That would mean that his last words were to something not chained to the physical world. I would like to think, for his sake and mine, that in the end I won our ongoing argument.

He was given a Talles (a Jewish prayer shawl) in his latter days by his son-in-law rabbi. I doubt he ever used it. It was the only thing of his Earthly possessions that I wanted. Every night, in front of a candle, I wrap myself in it and meditate and pray. It always gives me a sense of connection with him.

Whether he likes it or not.

Death of a Friend

Gerry Kruger

I am a huge fan of the Virginia Cavaliers (also known as Wahoos), so naming a pair of Canada geese Wah and Hoo was a significant tribute from me. From the beginning Wah and Hoo were gentle and respectful. They never hissed at me no matter how long they had to wait for their daily allotment of corn. They even obeyed my no-sitting-in-the-driveway rule. As a result, I rarely had to clean up after them. As far as I knew, this would be their first hatch, and I was sure they would be excellent parents.

During most of the nesting period, Wah went without eating so their eggs wouldn't be left unattended. Once every two or three days Hoo escorted her up to the corn I threw to them. She attacked it like a starving prisoner given real food for the first time in months. "Poor Wah," I'd say to her. "You're going to be a great mother, but you're got to eat more often, so you'll be strong enough to care for the new additions." She'd continue to gobble her corn nonstop—then hurry back to the nest.

* * * *

Riotous honking awakened me at three o'clock in the morning. I turned on the outside lights and spied a white four-footed creature a few feet from Wah's nest. Was it a dog? Wah had deserted her nest and was honking from the water with Hoo. I was sure they would lose or had already lost their eggs. I flashed the outside lights on and off, on and off, on and off. Was that enough to scare off the outlaw dog, or whatever it was? I saw it back up and leave the scene.

Satisfied that I had disrupted the looting of the nest, I left the lights on and went back to bed. More honking. Had the marauder returned? The geese quieted down. Still wondering if there was anything I could do, I went back to sleep.

I awoke with a start and realized it was morning. I fumbled for the opera glasses in the cabinet next to my bed and looked out the bedroom window for the geese. The binoculars were downstairs on the screen porch, but I wanted to check on the geese immediately. There was something in the field near the nest that I hadn't seen before. The opera glasses confirmed that the grayish mass could be goose feathers. In an instant I dressed and hurried downstairs for the binoculars on the screen porch. My heart dropped to my stomach. The pile in question was more than a scattering of feathers. It was large. And worse, I could only see one goose in the water and no one sitting on the nest.

Now I was walking toward the pile of feathers near the nest. There were five undisturbed eggs. It was my first look at them. I've learned that geese don't want anyone near their nests, and I respect their wishes. One egg was separated from the others, but they were intact. The one goose in the water was clearly deserting the nest, which convinced me that the creature I saw had spoiled it. Perhaps it had also moved the egg that was separated from the others. I thought about pitching the remaining eggs into the water, so it couldn't come back and eat them. But then I thought that Wah might decide to come back to the nest after all.

I took a deep breath and knelt next to the feathers. My eyes moved slowly over them. There were some rather large clumps of feathers, and then I saw the unthinkable . . . Hoo's head had been ripped off. No signs of the rest of his body. The killer must have carried off the rest of Hoo.

I looked at Wah and cried. "I'm so sorry. I'm so sorry," was all I could say. Wah was quiet and seemed to feel my grief.

I knew I had to bury him. Carrying a snow shovel, rake, and cardboard box, I approached Hoo's remains reverently and began scooping up the feathers and putting them in the box. Finally I put down the rake and shovel and lovingly held his head in my hands. "You were a brave and loyal goose," I said as the tears poured down my face. "You were a brave and loyal goose."

I planted a young, healthy Echinacea plant above Hoo as I eulogized him. Its pink petals and dark brown centers will sprout above the dark green foliage and come back every year. Rain began to fall and I sang to him for the last time, "A little drop of rain will hardly hurt you now, and rain will make the flowers grow."

When I remember the geese I have cared for over the years, I sometimes wonder if I have been wrong to become so involved in their lives. Did feeding them make them too dependent on me and too tame to survive predators? I like having the geese around. I like the male looking hard at me until I spot his mate sitting on a freshly made nest for the first time. I like talking to them and knowing that they recognize my voice. I like the way they stop whatever they're doing, tilt their heads, and listen when I sing to them. I like knowing that they trust me above other humans. I can't imagine the pond without geese. I'd miss their arrival in spring. I'd miss hearing their honking for breakfast when I wake up in the morning. The geese enrich my life. I hope I've made their lives richer too.

Keeping in Touch and Finding Patience

Gary D. Kessler

A legend in my family is that Grandmother Etta ran down the one street of Dixon, Wyoming, on the Colorado border, the day after Thanksgiving Day in 1944, laughing and skipping, waving a telegram, and calling out, "George has been shot! George has been shot!" As postmistress of Dixon, she had been the one to receive the telegram from the War Department. George was Etta's youngest son.

Etta's daughter-in-law, George's wife, Velma, ran along behind her explaining to everyone who had popped out of their houses to get a load of Etta's dance down the dirt road that George was alive, which was the reason for the celebration, and that the telegram had said the wound was "slight." (As "slight" as the wound was, a bullet passing through both calves of his legs, the same wound produced a blood clot that went to George's heart thirty-nine years later as he was reading the morning paper and killed him instantly.)

The text of the telegram, sent from Washington, D.C., and addressed to Velma Kessler, read, "Regret to inform you your husband George D. Kessler was slightly wounded in action 31 Oct. in France. You will be advised as reports of condition are received."

The news reached Velma three and a half weeks after the event. What was more notable—and a justification for Etta's dance down Dixon's only street—was that it was the first indication in eleven months of thinking otherwise that Velma and her mother-in-law had that George was even alive. He had previously been reported missing in action in an early February 1944, multiday battle, at the Caves of Pozzolana, north of Naples, during the Allied invasion of Italy at Anzio. As a member of what United Press in a 23 February 1944 article called the "Lost Battalion" of World War II, George had been declared among the 550 missing, presumed dead, of a 700-man battalion.

Although George survived that battle, bringing a medical unit with wounded soldiers safely to Allied lines, and was awarded the Silver Star in May of 1944 for having done that, word of his survival had never reached Wyoming. During that war, War Department notifications were spotty, at best, and soldiers were permitted no contact with their families—in letters home—during combat. This was determined necessary in that war to deny the enemy any possible knowledge of troop locations, unit affiliations, unit strengths, and possible routes of attack.

The first direct word of any sort that the Kessler family in Wyoming—his wife, Velma; his mother, Etta; and George and Velma's daughter, born in December, 1942—received since George arrived in North Africa in June of 1943, was the November 1944 telegram of his wounding in October of that year. They knew he was in the 157th Regiment of the 45th (Thunderbird) Infantry Division. And they knew from rare press reports at the time that his division had landed in Sicily in July of 1943 and at Anzio, on the Italian mainland, in January of 1944. The next they knew from press reports—made public because the losses were so catastrophic—was of more than three-quarters of George's battalion having died or been declared missing in fighting north of Naples.

To add to this, the November 1944 telegram was the last news his family had directly about him until, having returned to his unit as it pushed into Germany, he participated in the liberation of Munich in May 1945 and was, for the first time, permitted to write home.

Flash forward seventy years. We have an entirely different world now in respect to connections between our soldiers serving overseas, even in combat zones, and their families at home. We still have soldiers in combat abroad, although the whole nature of war has changed in the last seventy years. But they no longer are isolated, either naturally or on purpose, as they were before. Through e-mail service, wide coverage of cell towers, cell phones that take and can send photos via the Internet, and Skype technology, we have almost instantaneous contact capacity across the globe, including into combat zones where American soldiers are serving. In today's world, soldiers are able to connect with their families nearly daily.

The change has come not just because the government is more concerned with the morale of soldiers and their families now than they were seventy years ago but also because advances in communications and transportation technology and links have exploded the idea that troop movements and dispositions can be kept secret anymore. We have overhead surveillance systems that have been able to erase the privacy of outdoor latrines, not less coalescing of troops and their movements, since the Cuban missile crisis of 1962. And, to the current consternation of many, we have signals intelligence capability that can isolate and pluck conversations out of the air from almost anywhere and decrypt them, as necessary, before those talking to each other can cut the connection.

This example of the change in communications capabilities between American soldiers abroad and their families at home in the last seven decades is indicative of how far we have come in being able to control our environment. But it also points, I believe, to how much control over our environment we expect and demand—and how impatient we can get when we don't have instantaneous satisfaction. As smart as we are in gaining and maintaining control, we still aren't smart enough to have everything we want, know everything we think we need to know, know where everything is, and control and prevent all catastrophic events, whether caused by humankind or by nature.

It's great to be able to talk, face to face, with your soldier son or spouse half way across the globe every day, but how quickly impatience and blame can surface if either communications breakdowns or the sudden need to go silent on operations close down on those connections for several days. It's times like this that it would be good to think back to the soldiers in World War II—or even as recently as Vietnam—to appreciate what *is* normally possible now in maintaining connections that once wasn't remotely possible.

These overreaching expectations and impatience with services and capabilities have easily spread to other areas of our daily lives in the age of racing technology. We expect to know and control everything just because we have so rapidly expanded the knowledge and capabilities that we do have.

Perhaps it's time to stop and acknowledge that we aren't really God. We can prepare for but not prevent tornadoes, we can't prevent every 9/11-type act of terrorism, we have no God-given right to know where, at the bottom of the ocean, every airliner that falls out of the sky is located—or even why it fell out of the sky. We are actually pretty good at handling all of this—and we are getting better at it all the time. But we don't get there "by personal right" to know everything.

And perhaps if we occasionally stop and look at how much better we are at it now than we were as little as seventy years ago, we will become a little more patient with our expectations and what we consider are our "rights" to information and constant contact with others (perhaps, just maybe, for example, we will be willing to just turn our cell phones off for the twenty-minute drive home from the office)—and we will be more appreciative of those who are making what we *can* know possible.

Such frustrations as not knowing for the longest time where Malaysia Air Flight 370 is and why it got there might be a bit less frustrating if we accept that we are not "owed" explanations and that we may never receive them because the universe—and even the Earth—are a bit larger and more complex than we can as yet control. Putting ourselves back in proper perspective this way may also help us appreciate just how awe inspiring the capabilities that we *have* been able to develop are—through the intelligence, dedication, and ongoing efforts of the folks who work these systems day in and day out, none of whom are using an Easy Button to get it done.

ON WRITING AND PUBLISHING

Liberating the Big Bat

Deborah M. Prum

Every day my mind feels like a big bat trapped in a tiny attic. Random thoughts keep bubbling up but then bang against those attic walls of "Keep on track. Focus on your task list."

If you are in the implementation stage of some project, you really do need to buck up and focus. However, if you're at the beginning of an endeavor, perhaps you'd benefit by harnessing that bubbling creative energy instead of fighting it.

I'm taking an improvisation class. One of our exercises is called "A" to "C" thinking. We form a circle. Then one person turns to his neighbor and says a word, any word. His neighbor quickly responds **not** with the first word that comes to her mind, but the second or third or even maybe fourth word. Then she turns to her neighbor with a new word.

For example, John says "Dog" to Sue. Sue thinks cat, mouse, Mickey Mouse, and then responds, "Walt Disney." Next, she turns to her neighbor and says, "Slippers," and the game continues.

This exercise forces you to think past your first knee-jerk response. You wind up exploring in all directions. Usually, those tangents are more interesting than your first response.

In life we often are told to get our little selves from point A to point B with NO DETOURS. Yet, even as we try desperately to stay on task, our minds are full of INTERESTING DETOURS. These detours can become the starting points of many a creative and innovative undertaking.

A to C thinking is at the heart of humor. When you say or write something that places two incongruent elements together, people laugh. And humor is a splendid way to attract and engage your audience. The essays in my audiobook, *First Kiss and Other Cautionary Tales*, employ the elements of unexpectedness and incongruence.

How do I come up with essay ideas? I grab onto a tiny detail: the way someone walks into a gym locker room, a broken-down car by the side of the road, the tone of a cop's voice. Then I take that detail and let my mind wander in all directions.

For example, the other day as I left the poorly designed parking lot of a new shopping plaza, I noticed two sets of cars almost get into fender benders. So, I started to think about what kind of person might have designed that dangerous lot. I came up with: (1) a designer who flunked out of engineering school, (2) a designer who's part of the Mob and has a vendetta against the shopkeepers in the plaza, or (3) *a designer who owns an auto body shop and wants to drum up some business.* So, by the time I've imagined the third possibility, I may have come up with a good opening line for a funny essay. (Okay, maybe not exactly hilarious, but give me some time to work on it.)

Here's another example. I've created an iBook called *Czars and Czarinas.* It's an interactive history of Russia for young adults. Admittedly, this is a tough sell—Russian history is not the sexiest of topics. So, while writing this book, I intentionally engaged in lots of A to C thinking, including lots of quirky humor. For example, Peter the Great hated Eudoxia, his first wife. Their marriage was a disaster. So, I placed a sound clip under a portrait of Eudoxia. When you click on the bar, you hear Eudoxia say (with a Russian accent), "The marriage, it was all Peter's fault."

In the iBook, I talk about Ivan the Terrible's elaborate efforts to find a wife. Next to his portrait, I include a personal ad: *Lonely Czar Seeks Wife: Loves long walks on the tundra, sipping borscht by a crackling fire, pillaging a village or two . . .*

So, sometimes you *do* have to stick to a plan in order to accomplish a task. However, at the beginning of a project, let your thoughts fly. Explore that second, third, or fourth idea beyond your initial response. Allow your mind to riff rhapsodically as you approach the creative challenges in your life. I guarantee you'll open new vistas.

Tip: How to Make Characters Lively

Deborah M. Prum

I take improv classes at The Big Blue Door. Recently, we learned a game called "Present, Past, Future." The exercise gave me wonderful insight in how to create characters who hop off of the page. Here's how it's played.

One person starts a scene as a particular character—shaping that character via words, actions, and appearance. A second person gets on stage and starts interacting with the first person, also shaping her character. Each actor strives to maintain her character's attitude and point of view throughout the scene. So, what results is two people on stage creating a situation. For example, a husband and wife arguing, or a child and teacher on a playground, or coworkers in an office.

Then, at some point, the director shouts out, "Past" (or "Future"). If it's past, the two actors immediately start creating a scene in the past, staying completely in the head of their character, same attitude/point of view/appearance, but now, in the "past," these characters get to portray the elements that helped to form the character we're already met in scene one.

Then, after scene two (in the past) runs for a bit, the director then shouts out, "Future." So, the two actors immediately must create a scene that encompasses the natural outcome of whatever it was that happened in scenes one and two, all the while staying completely in their own character's head, but also allowing for the changes that time might introduce into their character.

All of this happens in less than ten minutes. Tricky? Yes. Tough. Yes. You have to be flexible, thinking on your feet the whole time. Yet, you have to hold the course, constantly considering—who is my character, what would he do, what would he say, how would he change, yet stay consistent with, his attitudes and point of view?

So, this game is excellent training for us writers when we're about to put pen to page. Live in your character's head. Determine appearance, attitude, actions, point of view, and so forth. Figure out what in the past made your character who he is today. Figure out what he is today and, given that, where he's likely to end up in the future, accounting for the kinds of changes a person like him may make.

Sounds complicated? The game becomes easier with time. (Or, maybe I'm just starting to develop multiple personalities!) In any case, it is well worth the effort to try this exercise as you plunge into writing a new story.

The Monkey and the Basket: A Lesson in Problem Solving

Deborah M. Prum

A few years back, I read a study about monkeys and baskets. I don't remember the names of the researchers or where they worked, but here's the gist of what happened.

They split monkeys into two groups. Then they taught all of the monkeys how to open a straw basket by pulling up a latch and lifting the lid. Simple. All the monkeys became expert lid-lifters.

Next, researchers put bananas into the baskets of one of the groups of monkeys. Those monkeys watched the bananas being put into the baskets and knew they were there.

Now here is the fascinating part of the study. The non-banana group of monkeys continued to be able to unlatch and lift lids just fine. However, the banana in the basket group of monkeys wanted to get to those bananas so badly they completely forgot how to open the lids. Frantically, they tried chewing through the basket, smashing it against the wall, maybe jumping on it—I can't remember. But the point is that they were so overwhelmed by their desire to eat those bananas, they couldn't remember a simple task they'd already mastered.

OK, here's how I learned this lesson in my own Real Life. I've written a book about the first nine centuries of Russian history for kids. You might ask why I thought that would be such a great idea. Let's just say, it's a long story.

The book is humorous and anecdotal—I'm positive kids would like it. A couple of years ago, Apple came out with iBookAuthor, a template for an interactive book. I decided to enter my finished Russian book into the template and release it through iTunes as an interactive book that could be read on an iPad. Using the template, you could include video and audio clips, 3-D widgets, tables, graphs.

Of course, Apple claims that this template is easy to use, and maybe it is—especially for computer-literate people—but I spent over a year, using Very Bad Language, trying to fit my book into the template. Hour after hour I watched tutorials and then tried to enter my text and pictures, only to have them disappear in a poof when I hit some mysterious button.

I was about to give up when one night at about two in the morning (yes, I'm an insomniac), I began to play with the template. I opened a new template and created a crazy book by dragging and dropping all the stuff on my desktop. The opening video was of a small child passing gas. The cover page was of my husband and me in Hawaiian outfits. I created a table of fictitious historical figures, like Frederic the Slimy, the years they lived, and whether they were Naughty or Nice. I figured out how to include a clip of one son attempting to play a cardboard didgeridoo. All of a sudden, because I was "playing" and wasn't overwrought about achieving a specific goal, I began to understand the workings of iBookAuthor, well, maybe about 50 percent of the program.

My point: Once I relaxed, once I wasn't so worried about "the banana in the basket," I was able to let my mind do the work of understanding iBookAuthor.

Of late I've spent lots of time trying to learn new skills: building a Web site, creating book trailers, overseeing the design of book covers, learning to play mandola and banjo ukelele. I'm realizing that, rather than getting all tangled up in obsessing over results, I need to relax and playfully find joy in the process.

Living With Our Muses

Jody Hobbs Hesler

I was in my early twenties when I read Katherine Dunn's *Geek Love*, which might begin to explain this one weird dream I had. In it I'm back in college, living in a trailer that serves as some sort of on-campus housing. A knock comes at the door. I open it to a hunchback dwarf on Canadian crutches. She's carrying a clipboard with a petition on it and a pen. The petition is for the college to improve accessibility for the disabled. Won't I sign? When I take the pen, the dwarf dives for my ankles and grabs for all she's worth. I try to free myself every way I can think of, but she won't let go, and I don't want to do anything that will hurt her. Next, I'm seemingly awake and in a diner, recounting the dream to some friends. One of them says, "That was your Muse." And then I wake up for real.

Over the years, this image has come back to me thousands of times—partly because it was such a vivid dream, and also, who doesn't want to meet their Muse? But then, who wants their Muse to be a disabled dwarf who shackles herself to your ankles?

I do my best to live in gentle coexistence with this thing that grasps onto me and will not let go. It sounds crazy. Sometimes it feels crazy when conversations among imagined characters in my head drown out the world around me, or when I scramble to the bathroom in the middle of the night to scratch out notes for a story or novel (the bathroom light won't wake my husband), or when I drive past real intersections in my hometown where fictional tragedies took place—the details of these invented tragedies sometimes trumping the actual details of wherever I might be headed at that time.

I often wonder what my Muse would be like now, if I could see her again. Haven't I changed? Haven't I cultivated a friendlier, more emotionally balanced relationship with her by now? If we were to meet again, perhaps there would be no sense of desperation, no clawing need on her part or fear that I might have to hurt her to get away on my part. Maybe we would be genuinely happy to see each other. We might sit in the shade of a tree for a cup of chamomile tea with a backdrop of butterflies and bird song.

Isn't it pretty to think so? Except there is that ebbing tide, sucking urgency to our work. Part of what we do clutches to our insides and pulls us with it into whatever world we have inside us where all the magic happens. It is a lovely place, but butterflies and chamomile tea? It's more badass than that. Maybe I would be lucky to have that dream over again and have my Muse show up, exactly as she did before—clutching, demanding, needing me.

The Joy of Writing Groups

Linda Levokove

If you've never been a member of a writing group you don't know what you're missing. Where else can you bring some meager offerings of your elegantly scripted genius and be regaled with critiques, because, frankly, who else would even be bothered to listen in the first place?

Some of the advantages of writing groups:

> They're usually free;
> Sometimes there's coffee and cake;
> Maybe you can carpool;
> You don't have to be best friends with the others;
> You don't have to even like the others;
> The group can meet frequently or infrequently;
> If you hate it you can always quit;
> You don't have to sit all alone at your computer.

On a more serious note, writing groups motivate you to write more and hopefully better. You can't just show up with nothing to share.

Remember that the group represents every person who will ever read your work. It therefore behooves you to pay close attention to their critiques, especially when more than one person has found fault with the same thing. On the other side of the coin, by critiquing other people's work you become more astute in critiquing your own. In other words you will become more adept at recognizing problems in your own work and will have the ability to rectify them.

As an added advantage, you will have many opportunities to practice reading in front of others, and this experience will hone your skills when you read your outstanding and brilliant work to huge audiences that will hang on your every word.

ABOUT THE AUTHORS

Clifford Garstang's ("Cousin Barnaby Is Dead," fiction) novel in stories, *What the Zhang Boys Know*, won the 2013 Library of Virginia Literary Award for Fiction. His first book, *In an Uncharted Country*, a collection of linked short stories, won the Maria Thomas Prize for Fiction. His work has appeared in *Bellevue Literary Review, Blackbird, Virginia Quarterly Review, Cream City Review, The Tampa Review*, and elsewhere. In addition to an MA in English and a law degree, he holds an MFA in Creative Writing. He is the cofounder and editor of *Prime Number Magazine* and is also the editor of *Everywhere Stories*, a short fiction anthology.

Jody Hobbs Hesler ("Brave Girl," fiction; "Famine Cottages, Ireland 2009," poem; "My Dad's Last Gun," essay; "Living with Our Muses," writing/publishing) lives and writes in the foothills of the Blue Ridge Mountains. Her fiction, feature articles, essays, and book reviews appear or are forthcoming in *[PANK], Steel Toe Review, Valparaiso Fiction Review, Prime Number, Pearl, Potato Eyes Journal, A Short Ride: Remembering Barry Hannah* (VOX Press), PhoneFiction,com, *Charlottesville Family Magazine, The Blue Ridge Anthology, Skyline 2014* and *2015, Stealing Time: A Literary Magazine for Parents*, and other places. One of her stories was a Pushcart Prize nominee and several have won regional contests, including the Virginia Writers Club Golden Nib award and UVA's Writer's Eye contest, and appear in prize anthologies. She has enjoyed fellowships at the Virginia Center for the Creative Arts and has conducted writing workshops in area schools for students from third through twelfth grade.

Sarah Collins Honenberger's ("Gravity," fiction) novel, *Catcher, Caught*, is a Pen/Faulkner Foundation selection in its Writers in Schools program. Audio, German, and Korean editions have been released. With numerous short fiction awards and a fellowship from the Virginia Creative Arts Center, she appears regularly on literary panels and at book festivals. Her other novels include *Minding Henry Lewis* (2014), *Waltzing Cowboys* (2009), and *White Lies: A Tale of Babies, Vaccines and Deception* (2006).

Gary D. Kessler ("The Invisibles," fiction; "Keeping in Touch and Finding Patience," essay), a freelance book editor, is a former news agency managing editor, diplomat, newspaper columnist, theater critic, and movie consultant. His published works include a short story collection, *On the Downtown Mall*; volume editor for the two-volume *WritersNet Anthology of Prose* and the four-volume *Blue Ridge Anthology*; coauthor of a publishing reference, *Finding Go! Matching Questions and Resources in Getting Published*; and a mystery novel, *What the Spider Saw*, which was nominated for the 2013 Library of Virginia Fiction Award. He has won and/or placed in Virginia Writers Club annual contests, the UVa Art Museum's Writer's Eye prose contest, and *The HooK* short story contest. His poetry has appeared in the *Piedmont Virginian*. He also writes pen name mystery novellas and novels.

Phyllis R. Koch-Sheras, PhD ("Light in the Forest," essay) is a clinical psychologist and author, living and working in Charlottesville since 1974. She has coauthored several books, including *The Dream Sourcebook*, *Couple Power Therapy: Building Commitment, Cooperation, Communication and Community in Relationships*, and *Lifelong Love: Creating and Maintaining an Extraordinary Relationship*. Currently, she is writing a musical entitled "Therapy: the Musical." Phyllis is also a professional opera singer and watercolor artist. She has had several solo art exhibits in Charlottesville, which include poetry readings of her poems inspired by the paintings. She is married and has two grown children.

Gerry Kruger ("Death of a Friend," essay), a native Virginian, moved in 1979 from Richmond to the Charlottesville area. She taught English for twenty-seven years at Charlottesville High School. Since 2004 she has participated as a judge in the Writer's Eye Contest, sponsored by the University of Virginia's Fralin Museum of Art. As an essayist on National Public Radio, she detailed the adventures of a lame Canada goose that arrived at her pond on foot in 2000 and stayed with her for nine years. Her first book, *On Kruger Pond: Charlie's Story*, chronicles her unique relationship with this goose and his struggles and triumphs.

Gerry continues to write about the geese on Kruger Pond and hopes to publish a sequel to Charlie's story.

Jean Lancaster ("The Storm" and "Lucky," fiction; "Nana's Arms," essay) is collections manager of the Fralin Museum of Art at the University of Virginia and has a BA in journalism from the University of South Carolina. Her writing voice has evolved from research and stories on ancestors who were English settlers of Flowerdew Hundred Plantation and French Huguenots in Manakintown on the James River. Her nonfiction works, "Shattered" and "Tantilla," are published in 2013 *Blue Ridge Anthology of Prose and Poetry*. She won second prize for nonfiction for "Taking the Waters" in the Virginia Writers Club 2013 Summer Shorts Writing Contest as well as second prize for nonfiction for "Nana's Arm" and honorable mention in fiction for "Lucky" in the VWC's 2014 Summer Shorts contest. Her essay "Taking the Waters" is published in the *Skyline 2014* anthology.

Susan M. Lanterman ("Close Encounters of the Furry Kind," essay) writes human-interest stories for the Commentary section of *The Daily Progress* newspaper and has coauthored "On the Block," a real estate column published in *The HooK* newspaper. While in New Hampshire, she produced *PC Connection's Guide* and edited the *Mary Hitchcock Memorial Newsletter*. Upon moving to Charlottesville, she managed the online journal *Neurosurgical Focus* for the *Journal of Neurosurgery* for nine years. Susan is currently completing a young adult novel, "Hasta Luego, Santa Claus," which follows the antics of a teenager and his family of illegal immigrants. She is also writing a collection of short stories based on her Charlottesville B&B.

Sharon Leiter ("Before Your Surgery," "I am running away from your body," and "A Visit," poems) is the author of three volumes of poetry, *The Night Heart Knows Every Word*, *The Dream of Leaving*, and *The Lady and the Bailiff of Time*, as well as two literary studies, *Akhmatova's Petersburg* and *Critical Companion to Emily Dickinson*. Her poetry has appeared in *Atlanta Review*, *Cimarron Review*, *Georgia Review*, and *Virginia Quarterly Review*. She received a 1990 Virginia Award for Fiction and is poetry editor of *Streetlight*. She teaches literature at the University of Virginia in Charlottesville, where she makes her home.

Linda Levokove ("Shadows in the Sand," "My Child in the Moonlight," "Of Flesh and Roses," poems; "The Joy of Writing Groups," writing/publishing) is the author of two collections of poetry: *Walk On The Heart Side* and *Cabbages & Kings*. She is former vice president of the Blue Ridge Writers Chapter of the Virginia Writers Club, a member of the Poetry Society of Virginia and the Virginia Writers Club, which has presented her with a Special Award for Outstanding Service and Contribution to Poetry in Central Virginia. In addition, she has participated in The Charlottesville Festival of the Book, teaches a Poetry Critique Group at Olli/UVa, and has presented her poetry at several public venues. Presently Linda is working on a collection of poetry and short/short stories.

Sigrid Mirabella ("Howling Totem," "Heart of a Wolf," and "Outfoxed by the Moon," poems), originally from Long Island, New York, defines herself as a social hermit and hopeful skeptic living in rural uncertainty. Her works have won awards and have appeared in *The Blue Ridge Anthology, Mid-America Poetry Review, Long Island Pet Gazette, Lynchburg News and Advance, Dog Fancy, Woman's Day, Countryside, People Magazines*, and various Macmillan/Howell books. In her other life, she works for a humane society in Nelson County, Virginia.

Brenda Morris ("The Magic Sweatshirt," fiction) is a retired teacher. She lives with her husband in Central Virginia. She began telling stories to her mother before she started school, and her favorite stories are adaptations about her mother's youth. Brenda writes short stories, memoirs, and poetry.

Deborah M. Prum ("JFK, Daddy, and Me," fiction; "Liberating The Bat," "How to Make Characters Lively," and "The Monkey and the Basket: A Lesson in Problem Solving," writing/publishing) is the author of *Fatty in the Back Seat* (a young adult novel), *First Kiss and Other Cautionary Tales* (an audiobook collection of humorous essays that first aired on NPR-member stations), *Czars and Czarinas* (an anecdotal and interactive history in iBook format) and *Rats, Bulls and Flying Machines* (a print book about the Renaissance). Her award-winning short fiction has been published in many places, including *The Virginia Quarterly Review*, *The Blue Ridge Anthology*, and *The Sweetbay Review*. Her humorous essays appear in many places, including the *Washington Post*, and air on NPR-member stations. Her work can be seen at www.deborahprum.com.

Elaine Ruggieri ("Nun Run," fiction), former vice president of public relations at the University of Virginia's Darden School of Business, has lived in Albemarle County since 1964. Having written nonfiction prose throughout her career, she is now concentrating on fiction. Her short story, "Deep Quarry," was published in *The Blue Ridge Anthology 2009*, "Doomsday" and the poem, "Lost in Verse," in *The Blue Ridge Anthology 2013*, and "Playing Nightly," in *Skyline 2014*.

Elizabeth Doyle Solomon ("Garden Gems," "Sunday in Shenandoah," and "Night Rain," poems), a New Orleans native and retired teacher, began writing at age eleven and publishing at age thirteen. Now in her seventies, she reckons her poems total over 60,000. Elizabeth has published two poetry collections, *Season*s and *The Steering Wheel Poems*, written newspaper columns, and founded the *Central Virginia Leader* newspaper. Her recent awards for both poetry and prose have come from the Poetry Society of Virginia and the Blue Ridge Writers. She leads the Blue Ridge weekly poets' critique group, and her third book, *Journey West and Everywhere*, has been accepted for publication in 2016.

Olivia Stowe (volume editor; "Blue Christmas," fiction) lives and writes in Central Virginia. Stowe's specialty is cozy mystery novellas, which include a thus-far nine-volume series of Charlotte Diamond mysteries, the most recent of which was *Follow the Palm*. The Christmas-season short story, "Cassandra's Last Spotlight," adds to this series. She also is the author of the inspirational *Savannah* novella series. Stowe's standalone mysteries include *Fiddler's Rest*, *Restoring the Castle*, and *Final Flight*. Her inspirational Christmas short story collections are available in the *Spirit of Christmas* and *Christmas Seconds* anthologies.

Leonard Tuchyner ("Planting Seeds," "Morning Dove," poems; "My Father's World," essay) is a semiretired counselor, living in Central Virginia with his wife and two dogs. He maintains an active involvement in the local writing community, which includes participation in two writing critique groups and in the Blue Ridge Writers Chapter of the Virginia Writers Club. Although challenged by legal blindness, he continues to pursue Tai Chi and related forms of martial arts. Gardening is another passion that has captivated him for most of his seventy-three-year life. One of his most fulfilling endeavors is the facilitation of a Senior Center's Writing for Healing and Growth writing group. He has been in the winners' circle of the BRWC's yearly writing contest several times. His winning entries have included poetry, fiction, and nonfiction. He has also been a regular contributor to *The Blue Ridge Anthology*. Mr. Tuchyner has published essays, poetry, and short stories in *Dialogue Magazine* (for which he now is a columnist), *Magnets and Ladders*, *Nomad's Choir*, *Westward Quarterly*, and *Skyline 2014*. A poetry book, *A Journey to Elsewhere*, was published in 2014.

Erin Newton Wells ("The Price of a Pig," essay) teaches studio art at her school, The Drawing Room, in Charlottesville, Virginia. In addition to this, she writes poetry, fiction, and nonfiction. Her subjects often are influenced by her native East Texas or her adopted Virginia. She is the recipient of writing awards from the Academy of American Poets, the Fralin Museum, and the Blue Ridge Writers Chapter of the Virginia Writers Club.

Lauvonda Lynn M. Young ("Warring With Words," poem) is past president of the Blue Ridge Writers Chapter, Virginia Writers Club (VWC), and program chair, Annual Poetry Contest and Ceremony, Poetry Virginia, Poetry Society of Virginia. She has served as editor for two newsletters, *The Blue Ridge* and *Friends Focus* (Friends of the Library, Fluvanna County). She is author of the poetry collection, *Just a Woman*, and her poems have been published in *Young America Sings, National High School Anthology*; *Piedmont Virginian*; *Blue Ridge Parkway Celebration, Silver Anniversary Edition; Blue Ridge Anthology*; and *Skyline 2014*. Her poetry has placed in contests of the Poetry Guild, Piedmont Virginia Community College, the Blue Ridge Writers Chapter of the VWC, and Poetry Virginia. Lynn is a member of the Appalachian Author's Guild (Abington, Virginia), Blue Ridge Writers Chapter of the VWC, Poetry Virginia, and WriterHouse (Charlottesville, Virginia).

~

Skyline 2015 and *Skyline 2014* are available in paperback and e-book from Amazon, Barnes & Noble, Create Space, the Book Depository, KOBO, iTunes, Scrib'd, Oyster, and many other distributors.

Skyline 2014

www.ingramcontent.com/pod-product-compliance
Lightning Source LLC
Chambersburg PA
CBHW071601200626
46811CB00027BA/861